I0145192

Catskills

&

Hudson Valley

Essays

JOHN BURROUGHS

2013
New Street Communications, LLC
Wickford, RI

newstreetcommunications.com

Introduction © 2013
New Street Communications, LLC

All rights reserved under International and Pan-American
Copyright Conventions. Except for brief quotations for review
purposes, the Introduction may not be reproduced in any form
without the permission of New Street Communications, LLC.
The works of John Burroughs are in the public domain, as are all
interior illustrations. Cover photograph by Amanda Pratt.

Published February 2013 by
New Street Communications, LLC
Wickford, Rhode Island
newstreetcommunications.com

Contents

1

Introduction

Writing in *The Nation* (January 27, 1876), Henry James described John Burroughs as a "more humorous, more available, and more sociable Thoreau." Burroughs's close friend and mentor Walt Whitman called him an "Audubon of prose." Through a long life (1837-1921) Burroughs published some 28 books – most of these collections of nature essays, but also volumes encompassing literary criticism and natural philosophy. There were, as well, two biographies – *Notes on Walt Whitman as Poet and Person* (1867) and *John James Audubon* (1902). The Whitman book was the first of Burroughs's to see print, and the first book-length study of the poet ever published. It is pious, fervent and devotional. The Aububon book is much less so – a potboiler cranked out to raise some quick cash.

Raised in the Delaware County Catskills, Burroughs spent the bulk of his life in that region and in the Hudson Valley, where the struggling writer acquired a fruit farm at West Park, Esopus, NY in 1873. The farm – which he named *Riverby* and would eventually make over entirely into a vineyard for growing table grapes – sloped down to the Hudson from what is now Route 9W, with a view across the Hudson to upper Hyde Park and Bard Rock. Here he built a Tudor-style house which still stands, and eventually a bark-covered study overlooking the fields and water. Here he entertained such literary lights as Whitman and Oscar Wilde. Here Burroughs and his wife Ursula raised their son Julian. And here he wrote the bulk of his books up until about 1895. In that year he purchased several acres about two miles inland and built himself a small cabin retreat which he dubbed *Slabsides*. (A few years later, he also began using a small house on his old family homestead in the Catskills, at Roxbury, as a summer residence, naming it *Woodchuck Lodge*.)

Throughout his long career as a "literary naturalist," Burroughs incessantly honed in on nature as found right at his doorstep in the Hudson Valley/Catskills region. "Nature comes home to one most when he is at home;" he wrote, "the stranger and traveler finds her a stranger and a traveler also. One's own landscape comes in time to be a sort of outlying part of himself; he has sowed himself broadcast upon it, and it reflects his own moods and feelings; he is sensitive to the verge of the horizon: cut those trees, and he bleeds; mar those hills, and he suffers."

Burroughs's home region of the Hudson Valley and Catskills infused the vast majority of his hundreds of nature essays. Interestingly, however, he never became a true devotee of the great river itself. "Friends have often asked me," he wrote after building Slabsides, "why I turned my back upon the Hudson and retreated into the wilderness. Well, I do not call it a retreat; I call it a withdrawal, a retirement, the taking up of a new position to renew the attack, it may be, more vigorously than ever. I had been so long perched high upon the banks of the great river, in sight of all the world, exposed to every wind that blows, with a horizon-line that sweeps over half a county, that, quite unconsciously to myself, I was pining for a nook to sit down in." He said he sought just "a few acres of level, fertile land shut off from the vain and noisy world of railroads, steamboats, and yachts by a wooded, precipitous mountain. Life has a different flavor here. It is reduced to simpler terms; its complex equations all disappear."

Burroughs continued: "To a countryman like myself, not born to a great river or an extensive water-view, these things, I think, grow wearisome after a time. He becomes surfeited with a beauty that is alien to him. He longs for something more homely, private, and secluded. Scenery may be too fine or too grand and imposing for one's daily and hourly view. It tires after a while. It demands a mood that comes to you only at intervals. Hence it is never wise to build your house on the most ambitious spot in the landscape. Rather seek out a more humble and secluded nook or corner, which you can fill and warm with your domestic and home instincts and affections. In some things the half is often more satisfying than the whole. A glimpse of the Hudson River between hills or through openings in the trees wears better with me than a long expanse of it constantly spread out before me."

Elsewhere he wrote: "A small river or stream flowing by one's door has many attractions over a large body of water like the Hudson. One can make a companion of it; he can walk with it and sit with it, or lounge on its banks, and feel that it is all his own. It becomes something private and special to him. You cannot have the same kind of attachment and sympathy with a great river; it does not flow through your affections like a lesser stream. The Hudson is a long arm of the sea, and it has something of the sea's austerity and grandeur."

When Whitman visited, however, he found great romance in the river. "The river at night has its special character-beauties," he wrote. "The shad fishermen go forth in their boats and pay out their nets—one sitting forward, rowing, and one standing up aft dropping it properly—marking the line with little floats bearing candles, conveying, as they glide over the water, an indescribable sentiment and doubled brightness. I like to watch the tows at night, too, with their twinkling lamps, and hear the husky panting of the steamers; or catch the sloops' and schooners' shadowy forms, like phantoms, white, silent, indefinite, out there."

Perhaps ironically, Burroughs's son Julian (1878-1954) became a most devoted river-man. Returning from Harvard in 1902, Julian (at his parents' request) settled in to take charge of the vineyard, which he was to manage till the end of his life. He also became a noted local architect and builder, and served many years as the property manager for Standard Oil tycoon Oliver Hazard Payne, whose vast estate lay just a mile or two north of Riverby. Every spring Julian was abroad on the river, paying out his shad-nets, most likely the only Harvard-trained fisherman anywhere on the estuary. (To this day, nearly 60 years after his death, Julian's several hand-crafted shad boats, and a number of carefully folded nets, rest in a shed at Riverby, quietly awaiting his return.)

In a memoir of his father, Julian spoke bemusedly of Burroughs's tepid and sometimes nervous relationship with the Hudson. Speaking of the father he remembered from childhood, he wrote:

It is a joy to think of him as he was then, virile in body, full fleshed, active, leading in walking and skating and swimming—

what a flood of memories! What an interest he took in all the things I did, and how often a most active part. One day in May I had gone out with our one shot of shad net, and was to try an experiment. I had told Father that I would row a ways up the river and throw out the net and then row on up to the mouth of Black Creek and fish for perch, and when the tide turned would row out and take up the net, which would catch the flood slack not far above. What he thought I do not know, for he went to Dick Martin, an experienced shad fisherman, and told him what I was going to do. Dick hastened to tell him, in alarm, that what I intended was impossible, that there was a row of old stakes out from the black barn just below the mouth of Black Creek and that my net would get fast on these and I would lose it, and perhaps come to harm besides. So Father walked the two miles, hurrying up along the steep and rocky shore, and found me just coming out from the creek. He told me what Dick had said and got into the boat and we rowed out to the net, which was acting very queerly.

"You're fast now, boy, it's just as Dick said," he exclaimed as I rowed as hard as I could for the long line of buoys. Never can I forget the hour of alarm and distress, for me, that followed. The tide turned and the loitering flood gave way to the sweeping ebb, the dark water from the creek came rushing down on us, the buoys swirled and twisted in the running water and began to disappear one by one. We quickly got hold of the end and I picked up as much as I could; then Father got hold and tried to pull the net loose. He pulled and pulled until he literally pulled the stern of the skiff under water.

"You'll have to cut the net, it is the only way," he said finally, red- faced and panting, so we did cut the net, leaving a middle section there on the old stake in the bottom of the river. There is no denying that it was thoughtful of him to come, and that he had my safety and welfare at heart. Though I was always cautious and wise to the way of the river, something might have happened and my bones might be there beside the old stake—and what a lot I would have missed!—or as Father once so aptly expressed it: "I'm not afraid to die, but I enjoy so much living!"

Back in the 1970's, when I lived at Riverby while a student at SUNY New Paltz, Julian's eldest daughter Elizabeth Burroughs Kelley told me how before Julian died in December of 1954, he'd outspokenly mourned the fact that *his* Hudson – the fabled, majestic river of Washington Irving and Thomas Cole – had become an open sewer and a tidal swath of filth.

In his time, Julian's father was always wary about the rise of the American industrial state. "In this age of science we have heaped up great intellectual riches of the pure scientific kind," he wrote. "Our mental coffers are fairly bursting with our stores of knowledge of material things. But what will it profit us if we gain the whole world and lose our own souls? Must our finer spiritual faculties, whence come our love, our reverence, our humility, and our appreciation of the beauty of the world, atrophy? 'Where there is no vision, the people perish.' Perish for want of a clear perception of the higher values of life. Where there is no vision, no intuitive perception of the

8

great fundamental truths of the inner spiritual world, science will not save us. In such a case our civilization is like an engine running without a headlight. Spiritual truths are spiritually discerned, material and logical truths — all the truths of the objective world — are intellectually discerned. The latter give us the keys of power and the conquest of the earth, but the former alone can save us — save us from the materialism of a scientific age."

Visiting Pittsburgh with its smoke-belching steel mills and chemical-ravaged Monongahela in 1918, Burroughs came away horrified by what he saw, but also with a vision of how humankind might very well save itself from environmental disaster:

Pittsburgh is a city that sits with its feet in or very near the lake of brimstone and fire ... I think I got nearer the infernal regions there than I ever did in any other city in this country. One is fairly suffocated at times driving along the public highway on a bright, breezy August day. It might well be the devil's laboratory. Out of such blackening and blasting fumes comes our civilization. [It is appropriate that] weapons of war and of destructiveness should come out of such pits ...

We live in an age of iron and have all we can do to keep the iron from entering our souls. Our vast industries have their root in the geologic history of the globe as in no other past age. We delve for our power, and it is all barbarous and unhandsome. [I look forward to the day when] we come to the surface and above the surface for the white coal, for the smokeless oil, for the winds and the sunshine, how much more attractive life will be! Our very minds ought to be cleaner.

Will Burroughs's idealistic vision prevail? If it is to do so, then it is up to us to make it so.

Edward Renehan
Managing Director
New Street Communications, LLC
Wickford, RI
newstreetcommunications.com

10

Burroughs's rustic retreat Slabsides still stands within the John Burroughs Nature Sanctuary, West Park, New York.

11

A Sharp Lookout

One has only to sit down in the woods or fields, or by the shore of the river or lake, and nearly everything of interest will come round to him, — the birds, the animals, the insects; and presently, after his eye has got accustomed to the place, and to the light and shade, he will probably see some plant or flower that he had sought in vain for, and that is a pleasant surprise to him. So, on a large scale, the student and lover of nature has this advantage over people who gad up and down the world, seeking some novelty or excitement; he has only to stay at home and see the procession pass. The great globe swings around to him like a revolving showcase; the change of the seasons is like the passage of strange and new countries; the zones of the earth, with all their beauties and marvels, pass one's door and linger long in the passing. What a voyage is this we make without leaving for a night our own fireside! St. Pierre well says that a sense of the power and mystery of nature shall spring up as fully in one's heart after he has made the circuit of his own field as after returning from a voyage round the world. I sit here amid the junipers of the Hudson, with purpose every year to go to Florida, or to the West Indies, or to the Pacific coast, yet the seasons pass and I am still loitering, with a half-defined suspicion, perhaps, that, if I remain quiet and keep a sharp lookout, these countries will come to me. I may stick it out yet, and not miss much after all. The great trouble is for Mohammed to know when the mountain really comes to him. Sometimes a rabbit or a jay or a little warbler brings the woods to my door. A loon on the river, and the Canada lakes are here; the sea-gulls and the fish hawk bring the sea; the call of the wild gander at night, what does it suggest? and the eagle flapping by, or floating along on a raft of ice, does not he bring the mountain? One spring morning five swans flew above my barn in single file, going northward,—an express train bound for Labrador. It was a more exhilarating sight than if I had seen them in their native haunts. They made a breeze in my mind, like a noble passage in a poem. How gently their great wings flapped; how easy to fly when spring gives the impulse! On another occasion I saw a line of fowls, probably swans, going northward, at such a height that they appeared like a faint, waving black line against the sky. They must have been at an altitude of two or three miles. I was looking intently at the clouds to see which way they moved, when the birds came into my field of vision. I should never have seen them had they not crossed the precise spot upon which my eye was fixed. As it was near sundown, they were probably launched for an all-night pull. They were going with great speed, and as they swayed a little this way and that, they suggested a slender, all but invisible, aerial serpent cleaving the ether. What a highway was pointed out up there!—an easy grade from the Gulf to Hudson's Bay.

Then the typical spring and summer and autumn days, of all shades and complexions,—one cannot afford to miss any of them; and when looked out upon from one's own spot of earth, how much more beautiful and significant they are! Nature comes home to one most when he is at home; the stranger and traveler finds her a stranger and a traveler also. One's own landscape comes in time to be a sort of outlying part of himself; he has sowed himself broadcast upon it, and it reflects his own moods and feelings; he is sensitive to the verge of the horizon: cut those trees, and he bleeds; mar those hills, and he suffers. How has the farmer planted himself in his fields; builded himself into his stone walls, and evoked the sympathy of the hills by his struggle! This home feeling, this domestication of nature, is important to the observer. This is the bird-lime with which he catches the bird; this is the private door that admits him behind the scenes. This is one source of Gilbert White's charm, and of the charm of Thoreau's "Walden."

The birds that come about one's door in winter, or that build in his trees in summer, what a peculiar interest they have! What crop have I sowed in Florida or in California, that I should go there to reap? I should be only a visitor, or formal caller upon nature, and the family would all wear masks. No; the place to observe nature is where you are; the walk to take to-day is the walk you took yesterday. You will not find just the same things: both the observed and the observer have changed; the ship is on another tack in both cases.

I shall probably never see another just such day as yesterday was, because one can never exactly repeat his observation,—cannot turn the leaf of the book of life backward,—and because each day has characteristics of its own. This was a typical March day, clear, dry, hard, and windy, the river rumpled and crumpled, the sky intense, distant objects strangely near; a day full of strong light, unusual; an extraordinary lightness and clearness all around the horizon, as if there were a diurnal aurora streaming up and burning through the sunlight; smoke from the first spring fires rising up in various directions,— a day that winnowed the air, and left no film in the sky. At night, how the big March bellows did work! Venus was like a great lamp in the sky. The stars all seemed brighter than usual, as if the wind blew them up like burning coals. Venus actually seemed to flare in the wind.

Each day foretells the next, if one could read the signs; today is the progenitor of tomorrow. When the atmosphere is telescopic, and distant objects stand out unusually clear and sharp, a storm is near. We are on the crest of the wave, and the depression follows quickly. It often happens that clouds are not so indicative of a storm as the total absence of clouds. In this state of the atmosphere the stars are unusually numerous and bright at night, which is also a bad omen.

I find this observation confirmed by Humboldt. "It appears," he says, "that the transparency of the air is prodigiously increased when a certain quantity of water is uniformly diffused through it." Again, he says that the mountaineers of the Alps "predict a change of weather when, the air being calm, the Alps covered with perpetual snow seem on a sudden to be nearer the observer, and their outlines are marked with great distinctness on the azure sky." He further observes that the same condition of the atmosphere renders distant sounds more audible.

There is one redness in the east in the morning that means storm, another that means wind. The former is broad, deep, and angry; the clouds look like a huge bed of burning coals just raked open; the latter is softer, more vapory, and more widely extended. Just at the point where the sun is going to rise, and some minutes in advance of his coming, there sometimes rises straight upward a rosy column; it is like a shaft of deeply dyed vapor, blending with and yet partly separated from the clouds, and the base of which presently comes to glow like the sun itself. The day that follows is pretty certain to be very windy. At other times the under sides of the eastern clouds are all turned to pink or rose-colored wool; the transformation extends until nearly the whole sky flushes, even the west glowing slightly; the sign is always to be interpreted as meaning fair weather.

The approach of great storms is seldom heralded by any striking or unusual phenomenon. The real weather gods are free from brag and bluster; but the sham gods fill the sky with portentous signs and omens. I recall one 5th of March as a day that would have filled the ancient observers with dreadful forebodings. At ten o'clock the sun was attended by four extraordinary sun-dogs. A large bright halo encompassed him, on the top of which the segment of a larger circle rested, forming a sort of heavy brilliant crown. At the bottom of the circle, and depending from it, was a mass of soft, glowing, iridescent vapor. On either side, like fragments of the larger circle, were two brilliant arcs. Altogether, it was the most portentous storm-breeding sun I ever beheld. In a dark hemlock wood in a valley, the owls were hooting ominously, and the crows dismally cawing. Before night the storm set in, a little sleet and rain of a few hours' duration, insignificant enough compared with the signs and wonders that preceded it.

To what extent the birds or animals can foretell the weather is uncertain. When the swallows are seen hawking very high it is a good indication; the insects upon which they feed venture up there only in the most auspicious weather. Yet bees will continue to leave the hive when a storm is imminent. I am told that one of the most reliable weather signs they have down in Texas is afforded by the ants. The ants bring their eggs up out of their underground retreats, and expose them to the warmth of the sun to be hatched. When they are seen carrying them in again in great haste, though there be not a cloud in the sky, your walk or your drive must be postponed: a storm is at hand. There is a passage in Virgil that is doubtless intended to embody a similar observation, though none of his translators seem to have hit its meaning accurately:—

Saepius et tectis penetralibus extulit ova
Angustum formica terens iter:

"Often also has the pismire making a narrow road brought forth her eggs out of the hidden recesses" is the literal translation of old John Martyn.

"Also the ant, incessantly traveling the same straight way with the eggs of her hidden store," is one of the latest metrical translations. Dryden has it: "The careful ant her secret cell forsakes and drags her eggs along the narrow tracks," which comes nearer to the fact. When a storm is coming, Virgil also makes his swallows skim low about the lake, which agrees with the observation above.

The critical moments of the day as regards the weather are at sunrise and sunset A clear sunset is always a good sign; an obscured sun, just at the moment of going down after a bright day, bodes storm. There is much truth, too, in the saying that if it rain before seven, it will clear before eleven. Nine times in ten it will turn out thus. The best time for it to begin to rain or snow, if it wants to hold out, is about mid-forenoon. The great storms usually begin at this time. On all occasions the weather is very sure to declare itself before eleven o'clock. If you are going on a picnic, or are going to start on a journey, and the morning is unsettled, wait till ten and one half o'clock, and you shall know what the remainder of the day will be. Midday clouds and afternoon clouds, except in the season of thunderstorms, are usually harmless idlers and vagabonds. But more to be relied on than any obvious sign is that subtle perception of the condition of the weather which a man has who spends much of his time in the open air. He can hardly tell how he knows it is going to rain; he hits the fact as an Indian does the mark with his arrow, without calculating and by a kind of sure instinct. As you read a man's purpose in his face, so you learn to read the purpose of the weather in the face of the day.

In observing the weather, however, as in the diagnosis of disease, the diathesis is all-important. All signs fail in a drought, because the predisposition, the diathesis, is so strongly toward fair weather; and the opposite signs fail during a wet spell, because nature is caught in the other rut.

Observe the lilies of the field. Sir John Lubbock says the dandelion lowers itself after flowering, and lies close to the ground while it is maturing its seed, and then rises up. It is true that the dandelion lowers itself after flowering, retires from society, as it were, and meditates in seclusion; but after it lifts itself up again the stalk begins anew to grow, it lengthens daily, keeping just above the grass till the fruit is ripened, and the little globe of silvery down is carried many inches higher than was the ring of golden flowers. And the reason is obvious. The plant depends upon the wind to scatter its seeds; every one of these little vessels spreads a sail to the breeze, and it is necessary that they be launched above the grass and weeds, amid which they would be caught and held did the stalk not continue to grow and outstrip the rival vegetation. It is a curious instance of foresight in a weed.

I wish I could read as clearly this puzzle of the button-balls (American plane-tree). Why has Nature taken such particular pains to keep these balls hanging to the parent tree intact till spring? What secret of hers has she buttoned in so securely? for these buttons will not come off. The wind cannot twist them off, nor warm nor wet hasten or retard them. The stem, or peduncle, by which the ball is held in the fall and winter, breaks up into a dozen or more threads or strands, that are stronger than those of hemp. When twisted tightly they make a little cord that I find it impossible to break with my hands. Had they been longer, the Indian would surely have used them to make his bow-strings and all the other strings he required. One could hang himself with a small cord of them. (In South America, Humboldt saw excellent cordage made by the Indians from the petioles of the Chiquichiqui palm.) Nature has determined that these buttons should stay on. In order that the seeds of this tree may germinate, it is probably necessary that they be kept dry during the winter, and reach the ground after the season of warmth and moisture is fully established. In May, just as the leaves and the new balls are emerging, at the touch of a warm, moist south wind, these spherical packages suddenly go to pieces— explode, in fact, like tiny bombshells that were fused to carry to this point—and scatter their seeds to the four winds. They yield at the same time a fine pollen-like dust that one would suspect played some part in fertilizing the new balls, did not botany teach him otherwise. At any rate, it is the only deciduous tree I know of that does not let go the old seed till the new is well on the way. It is plain why the sugar-berry-tree or lotus holds its drupes all winter: it is in order that the birds may come and sow the seed. The berries are like small gravel stones with a sugar coating, and a bird will not eat them till he is pretty hard pressed, but in late fall and winter the robins, cedar-birds, and bluebirds devour them readily, and of course lend their wings to scatter the seed far and wide. The same is true of juniper-berries, and the fruit of the bitter-sweet.

In certain other cases where the fruit tends to hang on during the winter, as with the bladder-nut and the honey-locust, it is probably because the frost and the perpetual moisture of the ground would rot or kill the germ. To beechnuts, chestnuts, and acorns the moisture of the ground and the covering of leaves seem congenial, though too much warmth and moisture often cause the acorns to germinate prematurely. I have found the ground under the oaks in December covered with nuts, all anchored to the earth by purple sprouts. But the winter which follows such untimely growths generally proves fatal to them.

One must always cross-question nature if he would get at the truth, and he will not get at it then unless he frames his questions with great skill. Most persons are unreliable observers because they put only leading questions, or vague questions.

Perhaps there is nothing in the operations of nature to which we can properly apply the term intelligence, yet there are many things that at first sight look like it. Place a tree or plant in an unusual position and it will prove itself equal to the occasion, and behave in an unusual manner; it will show original resources; it will seem to try intelligently to master the difficulties. Up by Furlow Lake, where I was camping out, a young hemlock had become established upon the end of a large and partly decayed log that reached many feet out into the lake. The young tree was eight or nine feet high; it had sent its roots down into the log and clasped it around on the outside, and had apparently discovered that there was water instead of soil immediately beneath it, and that its sustenance must be sought elsewhere and that quickly. Accordingly it had started one large root, by far the largest of all, for the shore along the top of the log. This root, when I saw the tree, was six or seven feet long, and had bridged more than half the distance that separated the tree from the land.

Was this a kind of intelligence? If the shore had lain in the other direction, no doubt at all but the root would have started for the other side. I know a yellow pine that stands on the side of a steep hill. To make its position more secure, it has thrown out a large root at right angles with its stem directly into the bank above it, which acts as a stay or guy-rope. It was positively the best thing the tree could do. The earth has washed away so that the root where it leaves the tree is two feet above the surface of the soil.

Yet both these cases are easily explained, and without attributing any power of choice, or act of intelligent selection, to the trees. In the case of the little hemlock upon the partly submerged log, roots were probably thrown out equally in all directions; on all sides but one they reached the water and stopped growing; the water checked them; but on the land side, the root on the top of the log, not meeting with any obstacle of the kind, kept on growing, and thus pushing its way toward the shore. It was a case of survival, not of the fittest, but of that which the situation favored,—the fittest with reference to position.

So with the pine-tree on the side of the hill. It probably started its roots in all directions, but only the one on the upper side survived and matured. Those on the lower side finally perished, and others lower down took their places. Thus the whole life upon the globe, as we see it, is the result of this blind groping and putting forth of Nature in every direction, with failure of some of her ventures and the success of others, the circumstances, the environments, supplying the checks and supplying the stimulus, the seed falling upon the barren places just the same as upon the fertile. No discrimination on the part of Nature that we can express in the terms of our own consciousness, but cease-less experiments in every possible direction. The only thing inexplicable is the inherent impulse to experiment, the original push, the principle of Life.

The good observer of nature holds his eye long and firmly to the point, as one does when looking at a puzzle picture, and will not be baffled. The cat catches the mouse, not merely because she watches for him, but because she is armed to catch him and is quick. So the observer finally gets the fact, not only because he has patience, but because his eye is sharp and his inference swift. Many a shrewd old farmer looks upon the milky way as a kind of weathercock, and will tell you that the way it points at night indicates the direction of the wind the following day. So, also, every new moon is either a dry moon or a wet moon, dry if a powder-horn would hang upon the lower limb, wet if it would not; forgetting the fact that, as a rule, when it is dry in one, part of the continent it is wet in some other part, and *vice versa*. When he kills his hogs in the fall, if the pork be very hard and solid he predicts a severe winter; if soft and loose, the opposite; again overlooking the fact that the kind of food and the temperature of the fall make the pork hard or make it soft. So with a hundred other signs, all the result of hasty and incomplete observations.

One season, the last day of December was very warm. The bees were out of the hive, and there was no frost in the air or in the ground. I was walking in the woods, when as I paused in the shade of a hemlock-tree I heard a sound proceed from beneath the wet leaves on the ground but a few feet from me that suggested a frog. Following it cautiously up, I at last determined upon the exact spot from whence the sound issued; lifting up the thick layer of leaves, there sat a frog—the wood frog, one of the first to appear in the marshes in spring, and which I have elsewhere called the "clucking frog"—in a little excavation in the surface of the leaf-mould. As it sat there the top of its back was level with the surface of the ground. This, then, was its hibernaculum; here it was prepared to pass the winter, with only a coverlid of wet matted leaves between it and zero weather. Forthwith I set up as a prophet of warm weather, and among other things predicted a failure of the ice crop on the river; which, indeed, others, who had not heard frogs croak on the 31st of December, had also begun to predict. Surely, I thought, this frog knows what it is about; here is the wisdom of nature; it would have gone deeper into the ground than that if a severe winter was approaching; so I was not anxious about my coal-bin, nor disturbed by longings for Florida. But what a winter followed, the winter of 1885, when the Hudson became coated with ice nearly two feet thick, and when March was as cold as January! I thought of my frog under the hemlock and wondered how it was faring. So one day the latter part of March, when the snow was gone, and there was a feeling of spring in the air, I turned aside in my walk to investigate it. The matted leaves were still frozen hard, but I succeeded in lifting them up and exposing the frog. There it sat as fresh and unscathed as in the fall. The ground beneath and all about it was still frozen like a rock, but apparently it had some means of its own of resisting the frost. It winked and bowed its head when I touched it, but did not seem inclined to leave its retreat. Some days later, after the frost was nearly all out of the ground, I passed that way, and found my frog had come out of its seclusion, and was resting amid the dry leaves. There was not much jump in it yet, but its color was growing lighter. A few more warm days, and its fellows, and doubtless itself too, were croaking and gamboling in the marshes.

This incident convinced me of two things; namely, that frogs know no more about the coming weather than we do, and that they do not retreat as deep into the ground to pass the winter as has been supposed. I used to think the muskrats could foretell an early and a severe winter, and have so written. But I am now convinced they cannot; they know as little about it as I do. Sometimes on an early and severe frost they seem to get alarmed and go to building their houses, but usually they seem to build early or late, high or low, just as the whim takes them.

In most of the operations of nature there is at least one unknown quantity; to find the exact value of this unknown factor is not so easy. The wool of the sheep, the fur of the animals, the feathers of the fowls, the husks of the maize, why are they thicker some seasons than others; what is the value of the unknown quantity her? Does it indicate a severe winter approaching? Only observations extending over a series of years could determine the point. How much patient observation it takes to settle many of the facts in the lives of the birds, animals, and insects! Gilbert White was all his life trying to determine whether or not swallows passed the winter in a torpid state in the mud at the bottom of ponds and marshes, and he died ignorant of the truth that they do not. Do honey-bees injure the grape and other fruits by puncturing the skin for the juice? The most patient watching by many skilled eyes all over the country has not yet settled the point. For my own part, I am convinced that they do not. The honey-bee is not the rough-and-ready freebooter that the wasp and bumblebee are; she has somewhat of feminine timidity, and leaves the first rude assaults to them. I knew the honey-bee was very fond of the locust blossoms, and that the trees hummed like a hive in the height of their flowering, but I did not know that the bumblebee was ever the sapper and miner that went ahead in this enterprise, till one day I placed myself amid the foliage of a locust and saw him savagely bite through the shank of the flower and extract the nectar, followed by a honey-bee that in every instance searched for this opening, and probed long and carefully for the leavings of her burly purveyor. The bumblebee rifles the dicentra and the columbine of their treasures in the same manner, namely, by slitting their pockets from the outside, and the honey-bee gleans after him, taking the small change he leaves. In the case of the locust, however, she usually obtains the honey without the aid of the larger bee.

Speaking of the honey-bee reminds me that the subtle and sleight-of-hand manner in which she fills her baskets with pollen and propolis is characteristic of much of Nature's doings. See the bee going from flower to flower with the golden pellets on her thighs, slowly and mysteriously increasing in size. If the miller were to take the toll of the grist he grinds by gathering the particles of flour from his coat and hat, as he moved rapidly about, or catching them in his pockets, he would be doing pretty nearly what the bee does. The little miller dusts herself with the pollen of the flower, and then, while on the wing, brushes it off with the fine brush on certain of her feet, and by some jugglery or other catches it in her pollen basket. One needs to look long and intently to see through the trick. Pliny says they fill their baskets with their fore feet, and that they fill their fore feet with their trunks, but it is a much more subtle operation than this. I have seen the bees come to a meal barrel in early spring, and to a pile of hardwood sawdust before there was yet anything in nature for them to work upon, and, having dusted their coats with the finer particles of the meal or the sawdust, hover on the wing above the mass till the little legerdemain feat is performed. Nature fills her baskets by the same sleight-of-hand, and the observer must be on the alert who would possess her secret. If the ancients had looked a little closer and sharper, would they ever have believed in spontaneous generation in the superficial way in which they did; that maggots, for instance, were generated spontaneously in putrid flesh? Could they not see the spawn of the blow-flies? Or, if Virgil had been a real observer of the bees, would he ever have credited, as he certainly appears to do, the fable of bees originating from the carcass of a steer? or that on windy days they carried little stones for ballast? or that two hostile swarms fought each other in the air? Indeed, the ignorance, or the false science, of the ancient observers, with regard to the whole subject of bees, is most remarkable; not false science merely with regard to their more hidden operations, but with regard to that which is open and patent to all who have eyes in their heads, and have ever had to do with them. And Pliny names authors who had devoted their whole lives to the study of the subject.

But the ancients, like women and children, were not accurate observers. Just at the critical moment their eyes were unsteady, or their fancy, or their credulity, or their impatience, got the better of them, so that their science was half fact and half fable. Thus, for instance, because the young cuckoo at times appeared to take the head of its small foster mother quite into its mouth while receiving its food, they believed that it finally devoured her. Pliny, who embodied the science of his times in his natural history, says of the wasp that it carries spiders to its nest, and then sits upon them until it hatches its young from them. A little careful observation would have shown him that this was only a half truth; that the whole truth was, that the spiders were entombed with the egg of the wasp to serve as food for the young when the egg shall have hatched.

What curious questions Plutarch discusses, as, for instance, "What is the reason that a bucket of water drawn out of a well, if it stands all night in the air that is in the well, is more cold in the morning than the rest of the water?" He could probably have given many reasons why "a watched pot never boils." The ancients, the same author says, held that the bodies of those killed by lightning never putrefy; that the sight of a ram quiets an enraged elephant; that a viper will lie stock still if touched by a beechen leaf; that a wild bull grows tame if bound with the twigs of a fig-tree; that a hen purifies herself with straw after she has laid an egg; that the deer buries his cast-off horns; that a goat stops the whole herd by holding a branch of the sea-holly in his mouth, etc. They sought to account for such things without stopping to ask, Are they true? Nature was too novel, or else too fearful, to them to be deliberately pursued and hunted down. Their youthful joy in her, or their dread and awe in her presence, may be better than our scientific satisfaction, or cool wonder, or our vague, mysterious sense of "something far more deeply interfused;" yet we cannot change with them if we would, and I, for one, would not if I could. Science does not mar nature. The railroad, Thoreau found, after all, to be about the wildest road he knew of, and the telegraph wires the best aeolian harp out of doors. Study of nature deepens the mystery and the charm because it removes the horizon farther off. We cease to fear, perhaps, but how can one cease to marvel and to love?

The fields and woods and waters about one are a book from which he may draw exhaustless entertainment, if he will. One must not only learn the writing, he must translate the language, the signs, and the hieroglyphics. It is a very quaint and elliptical writing, and much must be supplied by the wit of the translator. At any rate, the lesson is to be well conned. Gilbert White said that that locality would be found the richest in zooelogical or botanical specimens which was most thoroughly examined. For more than forty years he studied the ornithology of his district without exhausting the subject. I thought I knew my own tramping ground pretty well, but one April day, when I looked a little closer than usual into a small semi-stagnant lakelet where I had peered a hundred times before, I suddenly discovered scores of little creatures that were as new to me as so many nymphs would have been. They were partly fish-shaped, from an inch to an inch and a half long, semi-transparent, with a dark brownish line visible the entire length of them (apparently the thread upon which the life of the animal hung, and by which its all but impalpable frame was held together), and suspending themselves in the water, or impelling themselves swiftly forward by means of a double row of fine, waving, hair-like appendages, that arose from what appeared to be the back,—a kind of undulating, pappus-like wings. What was it? I did not know. None of my friends or scientific acquaintances knew. I wrote to a learned man, an authority upon fish, describing the creature as well as I could. He replied that it was only a familiar species of phyllopodous crustacean, known as *Eubranchipus vernalis*.

I remember that our guide in the Maine woods, seeing I had names of my own for some of the plants, would often ask me the name of this and that flower for which he had no word; and that when I could recall the full Latin term, it seemed overwhelmingly convincing and satisfying to him. It was evidently a relief to know that these obscure plants of his native heath had been found worthy of a learned name, and that the Maine woods were not so uncivil and outlandish as they might at first seem: it was a comfort to him to know that he did not live beyond the reach of botany. In like manner I found satisfaction in knowing that my novel fish had been recognized and worthily named; the title conferred a new dignity at once; but when the learned man added that it was familiarly called the "fairy shrimp," I felt a deeper pleasure. Fairy-like it certainly was, in its aerial, unsubstantial look, and in its delicate, down-like means of locomotion; but the large head, with its curious folds, and its eyes standing out in relief, as if on the heads of two pins, were gnome-like. Probably the fairy wore a mask, and wanted to appear terrible to human eyes. Then the creatures had sprung out of the earth as by magic. I found some in a furrow in a plowed field that had encroached upon a swamp. In the fall the plow had been there, and had turned up only the moist earth; now a little water was standing there, from which the April sunbeams had invoked these airy, fairy creatures. They belong to the crustaceans, but apparently no creature has so thin or impalpable a crust; you can almost see through them; certainly you can see what they have had for dinner, if they have eaten substantial food.

All we know about the private and essential natural history of the bees, the birds, the fishes, the animals, the plants, is the result of close, patient, quick-witted observation. Yet Nature will often elude one for all his pains and alertness. Thoreau, as revealed in his journal, was for years trying to settle in his own mind what was the first thing that stirred in spring, after the severe New England winter,—in what was the first sign or pulse of returning life manifest; and he never seems to have been quite sure. He could not get his salt on the tail of this bird. He dug into the swamps, he peered into the water, he felt with benumbed hands for the radical leaves of the plants under the snow; he inspected the buds on the willows, the catkins on the alders; he went out before daylight of a March morning and remained out after dark; he watched the lichens and mosses on the rocks; he listened for the birds; he was on the alert for the first frog ("Can you be absolutely sure," he says, "that you have heard the first frog that croaked in the township?"); he stuck a pin here and he stuck a pin there, and there, and still he could not satisfy himself. Nor can any one. Life appears to start in several things simultaneously. Of a warm thawy day in February the snow is suddenly covered with myriads of snow fleas looking like black, new powder just spilled there. Or you may see a winged insect in the air. On the selfsame day the grass in the spring run and the catkins on the alders will have started a little; and if you look sharply, while passing along some sheltered nook or grassy slope where the sunshine lies warm on the bare ground, you will probably see a grasshopper or two. The grass hatches out under the snow, and why should not the grasshopper? At any rate, a few such hardy specimens may be found in the latter part of our milder winters wherever the sun has uncovered a sheltered bit of grass for a few days, even after a night of ten or twelve degrees of frost. Take them in the shade, and let them freeze stiff as pokers, and when thawed out again they will hop briskly. And yet, if a poet were to put grasshoppers in his winter poem, we should require pretty full specifications of him, or else fur to clothe them with. Nature will not be cornered, yet she does many things in a corner and surreptitiously. She is all things to all men; she has whole truths, half truths, and quarter truths, if not still smaller fractions. The careful observer finds this out sooner or later. Old fox-hunters will tell you, on the evidence of their own eyes, that there is a black fox and a silver-gray fox, two species, but there are not; the black fox is black when coming toward you or running from you, and silver gray at point-blank view, when the eye penetrates the fur; each separate hair is gray the first half and black the last. This is a sample of nature's half truths.

Which are our sweet-scented wild flowers? Put your nose to every flower you pluck, and you will be surprised how your list will swell the more you smell. I plucked some wild blue violets one day, the *ovata* variety of the*sagittata*, that had a faint perfume of sweet clover, but I never could find another that had any odor. A pupil disputed with his teacher about the hepatica, claiming in opposition that it was sweet-scented. Some hepaticas are sweet-scented and some are not, and the perfume is stronger some seasons than others. After the unusually severe winter of 1880-81, the variety of hepatica called the sharp-lobed was markedly sweet in nearly every one of the hundreds of specimens I examined. A handful of them exhaled a most delicious perfume. The white ones that season were largely in the ascendant; and probably the white specimens of both varieties, one season with another, will oftenest prove sweet-scented. Darwin says a considerably larger proportion of white flowers are sweet-scented than of any other color. The only sweet violets I can depend upon are white, *Viola blanda* and *Viola Canadensis*, and white largely predominates among our other odorous wild flowers. All the fruit-trees have white or pinkish blossoms. I recall no native blue flower of New York or New England that is fragrant except in the rare case of the arrow-leaved violet, above referred to. The earliest yellow flowers, like the dandelion and yellow violets, are not fragrant. Later in the season yellow is frequently accompanied with fragrance, as in the evening primrose, the yellow lady's-slipper, horned bladderwort, and others.

My readers probably remember that on a former occasion I have mildly taken the poet Bryant to task for leading his readers to infer that the early yellow violet was sweet-scented. In view of the capriciousness of the perfume of certain of our wild flowers, I have during the past few years tried industriously to convict myself of error in respect to this flower. The round-leaved yellow violet was one of the earliest and most abundant wild flowers in the woods where my youth was passed, and whither I still make annual pilgrimages. I have pursued it on mountains and in lowlands, in "beechen woods" and amid the hemlocks; and while, with respect to its earliness, it overtakes the hepatica in the latter part of April, as do also the dog's-tooth violet and the claytonia, yet the first hepaticas, where the two plants grow side by side, bloom about a week before the first violet. And I have yet to find one that has an odor that could be called a perfume. A handful of them, indeed, has a faint, bitterish smell, not unlike that of the dandelion in quality; but if every flower that has a smell is sweet-scented, then every bird that makes a noise is a songster.

On the occasion above referred to, I also dissented from Lowell's statement, in "Al Fresco," that in early summer the dandelion blooms, in general, with the buttercup and the clover. I am aware that such criticism of the poets is small game, and not worth the powder. General truth, and not specific fact, is what we are to expect of the poets. Bryant's "Yellow Violet" poem is tender and appropriate, and such as only a real lover and observer of nature could feel or express; and Lowell's "Al Fresco" is full of the luxurious feeling of early summer, and this is, of course, the main thing; a good reader cares for little else; I care for little else myself. But when you take your coin to the assay office it must be weighed and tested, and in the comments referred to I (unwisely perhaps) sought to smelt this gold of the poets in the naturalist's pot, to see what alloy of error I could detect in it. Were the poems true to their last word? They were not, and much subsequent investigation has only confirmed my first analysis. The general truth is on my side, and the specific fact, if such exists in this case, on the side of the poets. It is possible that there may be a fragrant yellow violet, as an exceptional occurrence, like that of the sweet-scented, arrow-leaved species above referred to, and that in some locality it may have bloomed before the hepatica; also that Lowell may have seen a belated dandelion or two in June, amid the clover and the buttercups; but, if so, they were the exception, and not the rule,—the specific or accidental fact, and not the general truth.

Dogmatism about nature, or about anything else, very often turns out to be an ungrateful cur that bites the hand that reared it. I speak from experience. I was once quite certain that the honey-bee did not work upon the blossoms of the trailing arbutus, but while walking in the woods one April day I came upon a spot of arbutus swarming with honey-bees. They were so eager for it that they crawled under the leaves and the moss to get at the blossoms, and refused on the instant the hive-honey which I happened to have with me, and which I offered them. I had had this flower under observation more than twenty years, and had never before seen it visited by honey-bees. The same season I saw them for the first time working upon the flower of bloodroot and of adder's-tongue. Hence I would not undertake to say again what flowers bees do not work upon. Virgil implies that they work upon the violet, and for aught I know they may. I have seen them very busy on the blossoms of the white oak, though this is not considered a honey or pollen yielding tree. From the smooth sumac they reap a harvest in midsummer, and in March they get a good grist of pollen from the skunk-cabbage.

I presume, however, it would be safe to say that there is a species of smilax with an unsavory name that the bee does not visit, *herbacea*. The production of this plant is a curious freak of nature. I find it growing along the fences where one would look for wild roses or the sweetbrier; its recurving or climbing stem, its glossy, deep-green, heart-shaped leaves, its clustering umbels of small greenish-yellow flowers, making it very pleasing to the eye; but to examine it closely one must positively hold his nose. It would be too cruel a joke to offer it to any person not acquainted with it to smell. It is like the vent of a charnel-house. It is first cousin to the trilliums, among the prettiest of our native wild flowers, and the same bad blood crops out in the purple trillium or birthroot.

Nature will include the disagreeable and repulsive also. I have seen the phallic fungus growing in June under a rosebush. There was the rose, and beneath it, springing from the same mould, was this diabolical offering to Priapus. With the perfume of the roses into the open window came the stench of this hideous parody, as if in mockery. I removed it, and another appeared in the same place shortly afterward. The earthman was rampant and insulting. Pan is not dead yet. At least he still makes a ghastly sign here and there in nature.

The good observer of nature exists in fragments, a trait here and a trait there. Each person sees what it concerns him to see. The fox-hunter knows pretty well the ways and habits of the fox, but on any other subject he is apt to mislead you. He comes to see only fox traits in whatever he looks upon. The bee-hunter will follow the bee, but lose the bird. The farmer notes what affects his crops and his earnings, and little else. Common people, St. Pierre says, observe without reasoning, and the learned reason without observing. If one could apply to the observation of nature the sense and skill of the South American *rastreador*, or trailer, how much he would track home! This man's eye, according to the accounts of travelers, is keener than a hound's scent. A fugitive can no more elude him than he can elude fate. His perceptions are said to be so keen that the displacement of a leaf or pebble, or the bending down of a spear of grass, or the removal of a little dust from the fence are enough to give him the clew. He sees the half-obliterated footprints of a thief in the sand, and carries the impression in his eye till a year afterward, when he again detects the same footprint in the suburbs of a city, and the culprit is tracked home and caught. I knew a man blind from his youth who not only went about his own neighborhood without a guide, turning up to his neighbor's gate or door as unerringly as if he had the best of eyes, but who would go many miles on an errand to a new part of the country. He seemed to carry a map of the township in the bottom of his feet, a most minute and accurate survey. He never took the wrong road, and he knew the right house when he had reached it. He was a miller and fuller, and ran his mill at night while his sons ran it by day. He never made a mistake with his customers' bags or wool, knowing each man's by the sense of touch. He frightened a colored man whom he detected stealing, as if he had seen out of the back of his head. Such facts show one how delicate and sensitive a man's relation to outward nature through his bodily senses may become. Heighten it a little more, and he could forecast the weather and the seasons, and detect hidden springs and minerals. A good observer has something of this delicacy and quickness of perception. All the great poets and naturalists have it. Agassiz traces the glaciers like a *rastreador*; and Darwin misses no step that the slow but tireless gods of physical change have taken, no matter how they cross or retrace their course. In the obscure fish-worm he sees an agent that has kneaded and leavened the soil like giant hands.

One secret of success in observing nature is capacity to take a hint; a hair may show where a lion is hid. One must put this and that together, and value bits and shreds. Much alloy exists with the truth. The gold of nature does not look like gold at the first glance. It must be smelted and refined in the mind of the observer. And one must crush mountains of quartz and wash hills of sand to get it. To know the indications is the main matter. People who do not know the secret are eager to take a walk with the observer to find where the mine is that contains such nuggets, little knowing that his ore-bed is but a gravel-heap to them. How insignificant appear most of the facts which one sees in his walks, in the life of the birds, the flowers, the animals, or in the phases of the landscape, or the look of the sky!—insignificant until they are put through some mental or emotional process and their true value appears. The diamond looks like a pebble until it is cut. One goes to Nature only for hints and half truths. Her facts are crude until you have absorbed them or translated them. Then the ideal steals in and lends a charm in spite of one. It is not so much what we see as what the thing seen suggests. We all see about the same; to one it means much, to another little. A fact that has passed through the mind of man, like lime or iron that has passed through his blood, has some quality or property super-added or brought out that it did not possess before. You may go to the fields and the woods, and gather fruit that is ripe for the palate without any aid of yours, but you cannot do this in science or in art. Here truth must be disentangled and interpreted, —must be made in the image of man. Hence all good observation is more or less a refining and transmuting process, and the secret is to know the crude material when you see it. I think of Wordsworth's lines:—

The mighty world
Of eye and ear, both what they half create and what perceive;

which is as true in the case of the naturalist as of the poet; both "half create" the world they describe. Darwin does something to his facts as well as Tennyson to his. Before a fact can become poetry, it must pass through the heart or the imagination of the poet; before it can become science, it must pass through the understanding of the scientist. Or one may say, it is with the thoughts and half thoughts that the walker gathers in the woods and fields, as with the common weeds and coarser wild flowers which he plucks for a bouquet,—wild carrot, purple aster, moth mullein, sedge, grass, etc.: they look common and uninteresting enough there in the fields, but the moment he separates them from the tangled mass, and brings them indoors, and places them in a vase, say of some choice glass, amid artificial things,—behold, how beautiful! They have an added charm and significance at once; they are defined and identified, and what was common and familiar becomes unexpectedly attractive. The writer's style, the quality of mind he brings, is the vase in which his commonplace impressions and incidents are made to appear so beautiful and significant.

Man can have but one interest in nature, namely, to see himself reflected or interpreted there; and we quickly neglect both poet and philosopher who fail to satisfy, in some measure, this feeling.

The Falling Leaves

The time of the falling of leaves has come again. Once more in our morning walk we tread upon carpets of gold and crimson, of brown and bronze, woven by the winds or the rains out of these delicate textures while we slept.

How beautifully the leaves grow old! How full of light and color are their last days! There are exceptions, of course. The leaves of most of the fruit-trees fade and wither and fall ingloriously. They bequeath their heritage of color to their fruit. Upon it they lavish the hues which other trees lavish upon their leaves. The pear-tree is often an exception. I have seen pear orchards in October painting a hillside in hues of mingled bronze and gold. And well may the peartree do this, it is so chary of color upon its fruit.

But in October what a feast to the eye our woods and groves present! The whole body of the air seems enriched by their calm, slow radiance. They are giving back the light they have been absorbing from the sun all summer.

The carpet of the newly fallen leaves looks so clean and delicate when it first covers the paths and the highways that one almost hesitates to walk upon it. Was it the gallant Raleigh who threw down his cloak for Queen Elizabeth to walk upon? See what a robe the maples have thrown down for you and me to walk upon! How one hesitates to soil it! The summer robes of the groves and the forests—more than robes, a vital part of themselves, the myriad living nets with which they have captured, and through which they have absorbed, the energy of the solar rays. What a change when the leaves are gone, and what a change when they come again! A naked tree may be a dead tree. The dry, inert bark, the rough, wirelike twigs change but little from summer to winter. When the leaves come, what a transformation, what mobility, what sensitiveness, what expression! Ten thousand delicate veined hands reaching forth and waving a greeting to the air and light, making a union and compact with them, like a wedding ceremony. How young the old trees suddenly become! what suppleness and grace invest their branches! The leaves are a touch of immortal youth. As the cambium layer beneath the bark is the girdle of perennial youth, so the leaves are the facial expression of the same quality. The leaves have their day and die, but the last leaf that comes to the branch is as young as the first. The leaves and the blossom and the fruit of the tree come and go, yet they age not; under the magic touch of spring the miracle is repeated over and over.

The maples perhaps undergo the most complete transformation of all the forest trees. Their leaves fairly become luminous, as if they glowed with inward light. In October a maple-tree before your window lights up your room like a great lamp. Even on cloudy days its presence helps to dispel the gloom. The elm, the oak, the beech, possess in a much less degree that quality of luminosity, though certain species of oak at times are rich in shades of red and bronze. The leaves of the trees just named for the most part turn brown before they fall. The great leaves or the sycamore assume a rich tan-color like fine leather.

The spider weaves a net out of her own vitals with which to capture her prey, but the net is not a part of herself as the leaf is a part of the tree. The spider repairs her damaged net, but the tree never repairs its leaves. It may put forth new leaves, but it never essays to patch up the old ones. Every tree has such a superabundance of leaves that a few more or less or a few torn and bruised ones do not seem to matter. When the leaf surface is seriously curtailed, as it often is by some insect pest, or some form of leaf-blight, or by the ravages of a hail-storm, the growth of the tree and the maturing of its fruit is seriously checked. To denude a tree of its foliage three years in succession usually proves fatal. The vitality of the tree declines year by year till death ensues.

To me nothing else about a tree is so remarkable as the extreme delicacy of the mechanism by which it grows and lives, the fine hairlike rootlets at the bottom and the microscopical cells of the leaves at the top. The rootlets absorb the water charge with mineral salts from the soil and the leaves absorb the sunbeams from the air. So it looks as if the tree were almost made of matter and spirit, like man; the ether with its vibrations, on the one-hand, and the earth with its inorganic compounds, on the other —earth salts and sunlight. The sturdy oak, the gigantic sequoia, are each equally finely organized in these parts that take hold upon nature. We call certain plants gross feeders, and in a sense they are; but all are delicate feeders in their mechanism of absorption from the earth and air.

The tree touches the inorganic world at the two finest points of its structure—the rootlets and the leaves. These attack the great crude world of inorganic matter with weapons so fine that only the microscope can fully reveal them to us. The animal world seizes its food in masses little and big, and often gorges itself with it, but the vegetable, through the agency of the solvent power of water, absorbs its nourishment molecule by molecule.

A tree does not live by its big roots—these are mainly for strength and to hold it to the ground. How they grip the rocks, fitting themselves to them, as Lowell says, like molten metal! The tree's life is in the fine hairlike rootlets that spring from the roots. Darwin says those rootlets behave as if they had minute brains in their extremities. They feel their way into the soil; they know the elements the plant wants; some select more lime, others more potash, others more magnesia. The wheat rootlets select more silica to make the stalk; the pea rootlets select more lime: the pea does not need the silica. The individuality of plants and trees in this respect is most remarkable. The cells of each seem to know what particular elements they want from the soil, as of course they do.

The vital activity of the tree goes on at three points - in the leaves, in the rootlets, and in the cambium layer. The activity of the leaf and rootlet furnishes the starchy deposit which forms this generative layer:the milky, mucilaginous girdle of matter between the outer bark and the wood through which the tree grows and increases in size. Generation and regeneration take place through this layer. I have called it the girdle of perpetual youth. It never grows old. It is annually renewed. The heart of the old apple-tree may decay and disappear, indeed the tree may be reduced to a mere shell and many of its branches may die and fall, but the few apples which it still bears attest the fact that its cambium layer, at least over a part of its surface, is still youthful and doing its work. It is this layer that the yellow-bellied woodpecker, known as the sapsucker, drills into and devours thus drawing directly upon the vitality of the tree. But his ravages are rarely serious. Only in two instances have I seen dead branches on an apple-tree that appeared to he the result of his drilling.

What we call the heart of a tree is in no sense the heart; it has no vital function, but only the mechanical one of strength and support. It adds to the tree's inertia and power to resist storms. The trunk of a tree is like a community where only one generation at a time is engaged in active business, the great mass of the population being retired and adding solidity and permanence to the social organism. The rootlets of a plant or a tree are like the laborers in the field that produce for us the raw material of our food, while the leaves are like our many devices for rendering it edible and nourishing. The rootlets continue their activity in the fall, after the leaves have fallen, and thus gorge the tree with fluid against the needs of the spring. In the growing tree or vine the sap, charged with nourishment, flows down from the top to the roots. In the spring it evidently flows upward, seeking the air through the leaves. Or rather, we may say that the crude sap always flows upward, while the nutritive sap flows downward, thus giving the tree a kind of double circulation.

A tree may be no more beautiful and wonderful when we have come to a knowledge of all its hidden processes, but it certainly is no less so. We do not think of the function of the leaves, nor of the bark, nor of the roots and rootlets, when we gaze upon a noble oak or an elm; we admire it for its form, its sturdiness, or its grace; it is akin to our-selves; it is the work of a vast community of cells like those that build up our own bodies; it is a fountain of living matter rising up out of tile earth and splitting up and spreading out at its top in a spray of leaves and flowers; and if we could see its hidden processes we should realize how truly like a fountain it is. While in full leaf a current of water is constantly flowing through it, and flowing upward against gravity. This stream of water is truly its life current; it enters at the rootlets under the ground and escapes at the top through the leaves by a process called transpiration. All the mineral salts with which the tree builds up its woody tissues,—its osseous system, so to speak,—the instruments with which it imprisons and consolidates the carbon which it obtains from the air, are borne in solution in this stream of water. Its function is analogous to that of the rivers which bring the produce and other material to the great cities situated upon their banks. A cloud of invisible vapor rises from the top of every tree and a thousand invisible rills enter it through its myriad hairlike rootlets. The trees are thus conduits in the circuit of the waters from the earth to the clouds. Our own bodies and the bodies of all living things perform a similar function. Life cannot go on without water, but water is not a food; it makes the processes of metabolism possible; assimilation and elimination go on through its agency. Water and air are the two ties between the organic and the inorganic. The function of the one is mainly mechanical, that of the other is mainly chemical.

As the water is drawn in at the roots, it flows out at the top, to which point it rises by capillary attraction and a process called osmosis. Neither of them is a strictly vital process, since both are found in the inorganic world; but they are in the service of what we call a vital principle. Some physicists and biochemists laugh at the idea of a vital principle. Huxley thought we might as well talk about the principle of aqueosity in water. We are the victims of words. The sun does not shoot out beams or rays, though the eye reports such; but it certainly sends forth energy; and it is as certain that there is a new activity in matter—some matter—that we call vital.

Matter behaves in a new manner; builds up new compounds and begets myriads of new forms not found in the inorganic world, till it finally builds up the body and mind of man. Death puts an end to this activity alike in man and tree, and a new kind of activity sets in—a disorganizing activity, still with the aid of water and air and living organisms. It is like the compositor distributing his type after the book is printed. The microorganisms answer to the compositor, but they are of a different kind from those which build up the body in the first instance. But the living body as a whole, with its complex of coordinating organs and functions-what attended to that? The cells build the parts, but what builds the whole?

How many things we have in common with the trees! The same mysterious gift of life, to begin with; the same primary elements—carbon, nitrogen, oxygen, and so on—in our bodies; and many of the same vital functions — respiration, circulation, absorption, assimilation, re-production. Protoplasm is the basis of life in both, and the cell is the architect that builds up the bodies of both. Trees are rooted men and men are walking trees. The tree absorbs its earth materials through the minute hairs on its rootlets, called fibrillae, and the animal body absorbs its nutriment through analogous organs in the intestines, called lacteals.

Whitman's expression "the slumbering and liquid trees" often comes to my mind. They are the words of a poet who sees hidden relations and meanings everywhere. He knows how fluid and adaptive all animate nature is. The trees are wrapped in a kind of slumber in winter, and they are reservoirs of living currents in summer. If all living bodies came originally out of the sea, they brought a big dower of the sea with them. The human body is mainly a few pinches of earth salts held in solution by several gallons of water. The ashes of the living tree bulk small in comparison with the amount of water it holds. Yes, "the slumbering and liquid trees." They awaken from their slumber in the spring, the scales fall from their buds, the fountains within them are unsealed, and they again become streams of living energy, breaking into leaf and bloom and fruit under the magic of the sun's rays.

Fishing for trout in Esopus Creek.

A Snow Storm

That is a striking line with which Emerson opens his beautiful poem of the Snow-Storm: —

Announced by all the trumpets of the sky,
Arrives the snow, and, driving o'er the fields,
Seems nowhere to alight.

One seems to see the clouds puffing their cheeks as they sound the charge of their white legions. But the line is more accurately descriptive of a rain-storm, as, in both summer and winter, rain is usually preceded by wind. Homer, describing a snow-storm in his time, says: — *The winds are lulled.*

The preparations of a snow-storm are, as a rule, gentle and quiet; a marked hush pervades both the earth and the sky. The movements of the celestial forces are muffled, as if the snow already paved the way of their coming. There is no uproar, no clashing of arms, no blowing of wind trumpets. These soft, feathery, exquisite crystals are formed as if in the silence and privacy of the inner cloud-chambers. Rude winds would break the spell and mar the process. The clouds are smoother, and slower in their movements, with less definite outlines than those which bring rain. In fact, everything is prophetic of the gentle and noiseless meteor that is approaching, and of the stillness that is to succeed it, when "all the batteries of sound are spiked," as Lowell says, and "we see the movements of life as a deaf man sees it,—a mere wraith of the clamorous existence that inflicts itself on our ears when the ground is bare." After the storm is fairly launched the winds not infrequently awake, and, seeing their opportunity, pipe the flakes a lively dance. I am speaking now of the typical, full-born midwinter storm that comes to us from the North or N. N. E., and that piles the landscape knee-deep with snow. Such a storm once came to us the last day of January,—the master-storm of the winter. Previous to that date, we had had but light snow. The spruces had been able to catch it all upon their arms, and keep a circle of bare ground beneath them where the birds scratched. But the day following this fall, they stood with their lower branches completely buried. If the Old Man of the North had but sent us his couriers and errand-boys before, the old graybeard appeared himself at our doors on this occasion, and we were all his subjects. His flag was upon every tree and roof, his seal upon every door and window, and his embargo upon every path and highway. He slipped down upon us, too, under the cover of such a bright, seraphic day,—a day that disarmed suspicion with all but the wise ones, a day without a cloud or a film, a gentle breeze from the west, a dry, bracing air, a blazing sun that brought out the bare ground under the lee of the fences and farm-buildings, and at night a spotless moon near her full. The next morning the sky reddened in the east, then became gray, heavy, and silent. A seamless cloud covered it. The smoke from the chimneys went up with a barely perceptible slant toward the north. In the forenoon the cedar-birds, purple finches, yellowbirds, nuthatches, bluebirds, were in flocks or in couples and trios about the trees, more or less noisy and loquacious. About noon a thin white veil began to blur the distant southern mountains. It was like a white dream slowly descending upon them. The first flake or flakelet that reached me was a mere white speck that came idly circling and eddying to the ground. I could not see it after it alighted. It might have been a scale from the feather of some passing bird, or a larger mote in the air that the stillness was allowing to settle. Yet it was the altogether inaudible and infinitesimal trumpeter that announced the coming storm, the grain of sand that heralded the desert. Presently another fell, then another; the white mist was creeping up the river valley. How slowly and loiteringly it came, and how microscopic its first siftings!

This mill is bolting its flour very fine, you think. But wait a little; it gets coarser by and by; you begin to see the flakes; they increase in numbers and in size, and before one o'clock it is snowing steadily. The flakes come straight down, but in a half hour they have a marked slant toward the north; the wind is taking a hand in the game. By mid-afternoon the storm is coming in regular pulse-beats or in vertical waves. The wind is not strong, but seems steady; the pines hum, yet there is a sort of rhythmic throb in the meteor; the air toward the wind looks ribbed with steady-moving vertical waves of snow. The impulses travel along like undulations in a vast suspended white curtain, imparted by some invisible hand there in the northeast. As the day declines the storm waxes, the wind increases, the snow-fall thickens, and

the housemates sit
Around the radiant fireplace, inclosed
In a tumultuous privacy of storm,

a privacy which you feel outside as well as in. Out-of-doors you seem in a vast tent of snow; the distance is shut out, near-by objects are hidden; there are white curtains above you and white screens about you, and you feel housed and secluded in storm. Your friend leaves your door, and he is wrapped away in white obscurity, caught up in a cloud, and his footsteps are obliterated. Travelers meet on the road, and do not see or hear each other till they are face to face. The passing train, half a mile away, gives forth a mere wraith of sound. Its whistle is deadened as in a dense wood.

Still the storm rose. At five o'clock I went forth to face it in a two-mile walk. It was exhilarating in the extreme. The snow was lighter than chaff. It had been dried in the Arctic ovens to the last degree. The foot sped through it without hindrance. I fancied the grouse and the quail quietly sitting down in the open places, and letting it drift over them. With head under wing, and wing snugly folded, they would be softly and tenderly buried in a few moments. The mice and the squirrels were in their dens, but I fancied the fox asleep upon some rock or log, and allowing the flakes to cover him. The hare in her form, too, was being warmly sepulchred with the rest. I thought of the young cattle and the sheep huddled together on the lee side of a haystack in some remote field, all enveloped in mantles of white.

I thought me on the ourie cattle,
Or silly sheep, wha bide this brattle
O' wintry war,
Or thro' the drift, deep-lairing sprattle,
Beneath a scaur.

    "Ilk happing bird, wee helpless thing,
That in the merry months o' spring
Delighted me to hear thee sing,
What comes o' thee?
Where wilt thou cow'r thy chittering wing,
And close thy ee?

As I passed the creek, I noticed the white woolly masses that filled the water. It was as if somebody upstream had been washing his sheep and the water had carried away all the wool, and I thought of the Psalmist's phrase, "He giveth snow like wool." On the river a heavy fall of snow simulates a thin layer of cotton batting. The tide drifts it along, and, where it meets with an obstruction alongshore, it folds up and becomes wrinkled or convoluted like a fabric, or like cotton sheeting. Attempt to row a boat through it, and it seems indeed like cotton or wool, every fibre of which resists your progress.

As the sun went down and darkness fell, the storm impulse reached its full. It became a wild conflagration of wind and snow; the world was wrapt in frost flame; it enveloped one, and penetrated his lungs and caught away his breath like a blast from a burning city. How it whipped around and under every cover and searched out every crack and crevice, sifting under the shingles in the attic, darting its white tongue under the kitchen door, puffing its breath down the chimney, roaring through the woods, stalking like a sheeted ghost across the hills, bending in white and ever-changing forms above the fences, sweeping across the plains, whirling in eddies behind the buildings, or leaping spitefully up their walls,—in short, taking the world entirely to itself, and giving a loose rein to its desire.

But in the morning, behold! the world was not consumed; it was not the besom of destruction, after all, but the gentle hand of mercy. How deeply and warmly and spotlessly Earth's nakedness is clothed!—the "wool" of the Psalmist nearly two feet deep. And as far as warmth and protection are concerned, there is a good deal of the virtue of wool in such a snow-fall. How it protects the grass, the plants, the roots of the trees, and the worms, insects, and smaller animals in the ground! It is a veritable fleece, beneath which the shivering earth ("the frozen hills ached with pain," says one of our young poets) is restored to warmth. When the temperature of the air is at zero, the thermometer, placed at the surface of the ground beneath a foot and a half of snow, would probably indicate but a few degrees below freezing; the snow is rendered such a perfect non-conductor of heat mainly by reason of the quantity of air that is caught and retained between the crystals. Then how, like a fleece of wool, it rounds and fills out the landscape, and makes the leanest and most angular field look smooth!

The day dawned, and continued as innocent and fair as the day which had preceded,—two mountain peaks of sky and sun, with their valley of cloud and snow between. Walk to the nearest spring run on such a morning, and you can see the Colorado valley and the great canons of the West in miniature, carved in alabaster. In the midst of the plain of snow lie these chasms; the vertical walls, the bold headlands, the turrets and spires and obelisks, the rounded and towering capes, the carved and buttressed precipices, the branch valleys and canons, and the winding and tortuous course of the main channel are all here,—all that the Yosemite or Yellowstone have to show, except the terraces and the cascades. Sometimes my canon is bridged, and one's fancy runs nimbly across a vast arch of Parian marble, and that makes up for the falls and the terraces. Where the ground is marshy, I come upon a pretty and vivid illustration of what I have read and been told of the Florida formation. This white and brittle limestone is undermined by water. Here are the dimples and depressions, the sinks and the wells, the springs and the lakes. Some places a mouse might break through the surface and reveal the water far beneath, or the snow gives way of its own weight, and you have a minute Florida well, with the truncated cone-shape and all. The arched and subterranean pools and passages are there likewise.

But there is a more beautiful and fundamental geology than this in the snow-storm: we are admitted into Nature's oldest laboratory, and see the working of the law by which the foundations of the material universe were laid,—the law or mystery of crystallization. The earth is built upon crystals; the granite rock is only a denser and more compact snow, or a kind of ice that was vapor once and may be vapor again. "Every stone is nothing else but a congealed lump of frozen earth," says Plutarch. By cold and pressure air can be liquefied, perhaps solidified. A little more time, a little more heat, and the hills are but April snow-banks. Nature has but two forms, the cell and the crystal—the crystal first, the cell last. All organic nature is built up of the cell; all inorganic, of the crystal. Cell upon cell rises the vegetable, rises the animal; crystal wedded to and compacted with crystal stretches the earth beneath them. See in the falling snow the old cooling and precipitation, and the shooting, radiating forms that are the architects of planet and globe.

We love the sight of the brown and ruddy earth; it is the color of life, while a snow-covered plain is the face of death; yet snow is but the mask of the life-giving rain; it, too, is the friend of man,—the tender, sculpturesque, immaculate, warming, fertilizing snow.

Wild Life in Winter

To many forms of life of our northern lands, winter means a long sleep; to others it means what it means to many fortunate human beings—travels in warm climes; to still others, who again have their human prototypes, it means a struggle, more or less fierce, to keep soul and body together; while to many insect forms it means death.

Most of the flies and beetles, wasps and hornets, moths, butterflies, and bumblebees die. The grasshoppers all die, with eggs for next season's crop deposited in the ground. Some of the butterflies winter over. The mourning cloak, the first butterfly to be seen in Spring, has passed the winter in my "Slabsides." The monarch migrates, probably the only one of our butterflies that does. It is a great flyer. I have seen it in the fall sailing serenely along over the inferno of New York streets. It has crossed the ocean and is spreading over the world. The yellow and black hornets lose heart as autumn comes on, desert their paper nests and die—all but the queen or mother hornet; she hunts out a retreat in the ground and passes the winter beyond the reach of frost. In the spring she comes forth and begins life anew, starting a little cone-shaped paper nest, building a few paper cells, laying an egg in each, and thus starting the new colony.

The same is true of the bumblebees; they are the creatures of a summer. In August, when the flowers fail, the colony breaks up, they desert the nest and pick up a precarious subsistence on asters and thistles till the frosts of October cut them off. You may often see, in late September or early October, these tramp bees passing the night or a cold rainstorm on the lee side of a thistle-head. The queen bee alone survives. You never see her playing the vagabond in the fall. At least I never have. She hunts out a retreat in the ground and passes the winter there, doubtless in a torpid state, as she stores no food against the inclement season. Emerson has put this fact into his poem on "TheHumble-Bee":

> When the fierce northwestern blast
> Cools sea and land so far and fast,
> Thou already slumberest deep;
> Woe and want thou canst outsleep;;
> Want and woe, which torture us,
> Thy slee makes ridiculous.

In early August of the past year I saw a queen bumblebee quickly enter a small hole on the edge of the road where there was no nest. It was probably her winter quarters.

If one could take the cover off the ground in the fields and woods in winter, or have some magic ointment put upon his eyes that would enable him to see through opaque substances, how many curious and interesting forms of life he would behold in the ground beneath his feet as he took his winter walk—life with the fires banked, so to speak, and just keeping till spring. He would see the field crickets in their galleries in the ground in a dormant state, all their machinery of life brought to a standstill by the cold. He would see the ants in their hills and in their tunnels in decaying trees and logs, as inert as the soil or the wood they inhabit. I have chopped many a handful of the big black ants out of a log upon my woodpile in winter, stiff, but not dead, with the frost, and brought them in by the fire to see their vital forces set going again by the heat. I have brought in the grubs of borers and the big fat grubs of beetles, turned out of their winter beds in old logs by my axe and frozen like ice-cream, and have seen the spark of life rekindle in them on the hearth.

With this added visual power, one would see the wood frogs and the hylas in their winter beds but a few inches beneath the moss and leaf-mould, one here and one there, cold, inert, biding their time. I dug a wood frog out one December and found him not frozen, though the Soil around him was full of frost; he was alive but not frisky. A friend of mine once found one in the woods sitting upon the snow one day in early winter. She carried him home with her, and he burrowed in the soil of her flower-pot and came out all right in the spring. What brought him out upon the snow in December one would like to know.

One would see the tree-frogs in the cavities of old trees, wrapped in their winter sleep—which is yet not a sleep, but suspended animation. When the day is warm, or the January thaw comes, I fancy the little frog feels it and stirs in his bed. One would see the warty toads squatted in the soil two or three feet below the surface, in the same way. Probably not till April will the spell which the winter has put upon them be broken. I have seen a toad go into the ground in late fall. He literally elbows his way into it, going down backwards.

Beneath rocks or in cavities at the end of some small hole in the ground, one would see a ball or tangle of garter snakes, or black snakes, or copperheads—dozens of individual snakes of that locality entwined in one many-headed mass, conserving in this united way their animal heat against the cold of winter. One spring my neighbor in the woods discovered such a winter retreat of the copperheads, and, visiting the place many times during the warm April days, he killed about forty snakes, and since that slaughter, the copperheads have been at a premium in our neighborhood.

Here and there, near the fences and along the borders of the wood, these X-ray eyes would see the chipmunk at the end of his deep burrow with his store of nuts or grains, sleeping fitfully but not dormant. The frost does not reach him and his stores are at hand. One which we dug out in late October had nearly four quarts of weed-seeds and cherry-pits. He will hardly be out before March, and then, like his big brother rodent the woodchuck, and other winter sleepers, his fancy will quickly "turn to thoughts of love."

One would see the woodchuck asleep in his burrow, snugly rolled up and living on his own fat. All the hibernating animals that keep up respiration, must have sustenance of some sort—either a store of food at hand or a store of fat in their own bodies. The woodchuck, the bear, the coon, the skunk, the 'possum, lay up a store of fuel in their own bodies, and they come out in the spring lean and hungry. The squirrels are lean the year through, and hence must have a store of food in their dens, as does the chipmunk, or else be more or less active in their search all winter, as is the case with the red and gray squirrels. The fox puts on more or less fat in the fall, because he will need it before spring. His food-supply is very precarious; he may go many days without a morsel. I have known him to be so hungry that he would eat frozen apples and corn which he could not digest. The hare and the rabbit, on the other hand, do not store up fat against a time of need; their food-supply of bark and twigs is constant, no matter how deep the snows. The birds of prey that pass the winter in the north take on a coat of fat in the fall, because their food-supply is so uncertain; the coat of fat is also a protection against the cold.

Of course, all the wild creatures are in better condition in the fall than in the spring, but in many cases the fat is distinctly a substitute for food.

The skunk is in his den also from December till February, living on his own fat. Several of them often occupy the same den and conserve their animal heat in that way. The coon, also, is in his den in the rocks for a part of the winter, keeping warm on home-made fuel. The same is true of the bear in our climate. The bats are hibernating in the rocks or about buildings. The muskrats are leading hidden lives in the upper chambers of their snow-covered houses in the marshes and ponds or in the banks of streams, feeding on lily-roots and mussels which they get under the ice.

The lean, bloodthirsty minks and weasels are on the hunt all winter. Our native mice are also active. That pretty stitching upon the coverlet of the winter snow in the woods is made by our white-footed mouse and by the little shrew mouse. The former often has large stores of nuts hidden in some cavity in a tree; what supply of food the latter has, if any, I do not know. In the winter the short-tailed meadow or field mice come out of their retreat in the ground and beneath stones and lead gay, fearless lives beneath the snow-drifts. Their little villages, with their runways and abandoned nests, may be seen when the snow disappears in the spring. Their winter life beneath the snow, where no wicked eye or murderous claw can reach them, is in sharp contrast to their life in summer, when cats and hawks, owls and foxes, pounce upon them day and night. It is only in times of deep snows that they bark our fruit-trees.

We have in this latitude but one species of hibernating mouse—the long tailed jumping mouse, or kangaroo mouse, as it is sometimes called from its mode of locomotion. Late one fall, while making a road near "Slabsides," we dug one out from its hibernation about two feet below the surface of the ground. It was like a little ball of fur tied with a string. In my hand it seemed as cold as if dead. Close scrutiny showed that it breathed at intervals, very slowly. The embers of life were there, but slumbering beneath the ashes. I put it in my pocket and went about my work. After a little time, remembering my mouse, I put my hand into my pocket and touched something very warm and lively. The ember had been fanned into a flame, so to speak. I kept my captive in a cage a day or two and then returned it to the woods, where I trust it found a safe retreat against the cold.

Winter Neighbors

The country is more of a wilderness, more of a wild solitude, in the winter than in the summer. The wild comes out. The urban, the cultivated, is hidden or negatived. You shall hardly know a good field from a poor, a meadow from a pasture, a park from a forest. Lines and boundaries are disregarded; gates and bar-ways are unclosed; man lets go his hold upon the earth; title-deeds are deep buried beneath the snow; the best-kept grounds relapse to a state of nature; under the pressure of the cold all the wild creatures become outlaws, and roam abroad beyond their usual haunts. The partridge comes to the orchard for buds; the rabbit comes to the garden and lawn; the crows and jays come to the ash-heap and corn-crib, the snow-buntings to the stack and to the barn-yard; the sparrows pilfer from the domestic fowls; the pine grosbeak comes down from the north and shears your maples of their buds; the fox prowls about your premises at night, and the red squirrels find your grain in the barn or steal the butternuts from your attic. In fact, winter, like some great calamity, changes the status of most creatures and sets them adrift. Winter, like poverty, makes us acquainted with strange bedfellows.

For my part, my nearest approach to a strange bedfellow is the little gray rabbit that has taken up her abode under my study floor. As she spends the day here and is out larking at night, she is not much of a bedfellow after all. It is probable that I disturb her slumbers more than she does mine. I think she is some support to me under there–a silent wild-eyed witness and backer; a type of the gentle and harmless in savage nature. She has no sagacity to give me or lend me, but that soft, nimble foot of hers, and that touch as of cotton wherever she goes, are worthy of emulation. I think I can feel her good-will through the floor, and I hope she can mine. When I have a happy thought I imagine her ears twitch, especially when I think of the sweet apple I will place by her doorway at night. I wonder if that fox chanced to catch a glimpse of her the other night when he stealthily leaped over the fence near by and walked along between the study and the house? How clearly one could read that it was not a little dog that had passed there. There was something furtive in the track; it shied off away from the house and around it, as if eying it suspiciously; and then it had the caution and deliberation of the fox—bold, bold, but not too bold; wariness was in every footprint. If it had been a little dog that had chanced to wander that way, when he crossed my path he would have followed it up to the barn and have gone smelling around for a bone; but this sharp, cautious track held straight across all others, keeping five or six rods from the house, up the hill, across the highway towards a neighboring farmstead, with its nose in the air and its eye and ear alert, so to speak.

A winter neighbor of mine in whom I am interested, and who perhaps lends me his support after his kind, is a little red owl, whose retreat is in the heart of an old apple-tree just over the fence. Where he keeps himself in spring and summer I do not know, but late every fall, and at intervals all winter, his hiding-place is discovered by the jays and nut-hatches, and proclaimed from the tree-tops for the space of half an hour or so, with all the powers of voice they can command. Four times during one winter they called me out to behold this little ogre feigning sleep in his den, sometimes in one apple-tree, sometimes in another. Whenever I heard their cries, I knew my neighbor was being berated. The birds would take turns at looking in upon him and uttering their alarm-notes. Every jay within hearing would come to the spot and at once approach the hole in the trunk or limb, and with a kind of breathless eagerness and excitement take a peep at the owl, and then join the outcry. When I approached they would hastily take a final look and then withdraw and regard my movements intently. After accustoming my eye to the faint light of the cavity for a few moments, I could usually make out the owl at the bottom feigning sleep. Feigning, I say, because this is what he really did, as I first discovered one day when I cut into his retreat with the axe. The loud blows and the falling chips did not disturb him at all. When I reached in a stick and pulled him over on his side, leaving one of his wings spread out, he made no attempt to recover himself, but lay among the chips and fragments of decayed wood, like a part of themselves. Indeed, it took a sharp eye to distinguish him. Nor till I had pulled him forth by one wing, rather rudely, did he abandon his trick of simulated sleep or death. Then, like a detected pickpocket, he was suddenly transformed into another creature. His eyes flew wide open, his talons clutched my finger, his ears were depressed, and every motion and look said, "Hands off, at your peril." Finding this game did not work, he soon began to "play 'possum" again. I put a cover over my study wood-box and kept him captive for a week. Look in upon him any time, night or day, and he was apparently wrapped in the profoundest slumber; but the live mice which I put into his box from time to time found his sleep was easily broken; there would be a sudden rustle in the box, a faint squeak, and then silence. After a week of captivity I gave him his freedom in the full sunshine: no trouble for him to see which way and where to go.

Just at dusk in the winter nights, I often hear his soft bur-r-r-r, very pleasing and bell-like. What a furtive, woody sound it is in the winter stillness, so unlike the harsh scream of the hawk. But all the ways of the owl are ways of softness and duskiness. His wings are shod with silence, his plumage is edged with down.

Another owl neighbor of mine, with whom I pass the time of day more frequently than with the last, lives farther away. I pass his castle every night on my way to the post-office, and in winter, if the hour is late enough, am pretty sure to see him standing in his doorway, surveying the passers-by and the landscape through narrow slits in his eyes. For four successive winters now have I observed him. As the twilight begins to deepen he rises out of his cavity in the apple-tree, scarcely faster than the moon rises from behind the hill, and sits in the

opening, completely framed by its outlines of gray bark
and dead wood, and by his protective coloring virtually
invisible to every eye that does not know he is there.
Probably my own is the only eye that has ever penetrated
his secret, and mine never would have done so had I not
chanced on one occasion to see him leave his retreat and
make a raid upon a shrike that was impaling a shrew-
mouse upon a thorn in a neighboring tree and which I was
watching. Failing to get the mouse, the owl returned
swiftly to his cavity, and ever since, while going that way,
I have been on the lookout for him. Dozens of teams and
foot-passengers pass him late in the day, but he regards
them not, nor they him. When I come alone and pause to
salute him, he opens his eyes a little wider, and, appearing
to recognize me, quickly shrinks and fades into the
background of his door in a very weird and curious
manner. When he is not at his outlook, or when he is, it
requires the best powers of the eye to decide the point, as
the empty cavity itself is almost an exact image of him. If
the whole thing had been carefully studied it could not
have answered its purpose better. The owl stands quite
perpendicular, presenting a front of light mottled gray; the
eyes are closed to a mere slit, the ear-feathers depressed,
the beak buried in the plumage, and the whole attitude is
one of silent, motionless waiting and observation. If a
mouse should be seen crossing the highway, or scudding
over any exposed part of the snowy surface in the twilight,
the owl would doubtless swoop down upon it. I think the
owl has learned to distinguish me from the rest of the
passers-by; at least, when I stop before him, and he sees

himself observed, he backs down into his den, as I have said, in a very amusing manner. Whether bluebirds, nut-hatches, and chickadees—birds that pass the night in cavities of trees—ever run into the clutches of the dozing owl, I should be glad to know. My impression is, however, that they seek out smaller cavities. An old willow by the roadside blew down one summer, and a decayed branch broke open, revealing a brood of half-fledged owls, and many feathers and quills of bluebirds, orioles, and other songsters, showing plainly enough why all birds fear and berate the owl.

The English house sparrows, that are so rapidly increasing among us, and that must add greatly to the food supply of the owls and other birds of prey, seek to baffle their enemies by roosting in the densest evergreens they can find, in the arbor-vitæ, and in hemlock hedges. Soft-winged as the owl is, he cannot steal in upon such a retreat without giving them warning.

These sparrows are becoming about the most noticeable of my winter neighbors, and a troop of them every morning watch me put out the hens' feed, and soon claim their share. I rather encouraged them in their neighborliness, till one day I discovered the snow under a favorite plum-tree where they most frequently perched covered with the scales of the fruit-buds. On investigating I found that the tree had been nearly stripped of its buds— a very unneighborly act on the part of the sparrows, considering, too, all the cracked corn I had scattered for them. So I at once served notice on them that our good understanding was at an end. And a hint is as good as a kick with this bird. The stone I hurled among them, and the one with which I followed them up, may have been taken as a kick; but they were only a hint of the shot-gun that stood ready in the corner. The sparrows left in high dungeon, and were not back again in some days, and were then very shy. No doubt the time is near at hand when we shall have to wage serious war upon these sparrows, as they long have had to do on the continent of Europe. And yet it will be hard to kill the little wretches, the only Old World bird we have. When I take down my gun to shoot them I shall probably remember that the Psalmist said, "I watch, and am as a sparrow alone upon the house-top," and maybe the recollection will cause me to stay my hand. The sparrows have the Old World hardiness and prolificness; they are wise and tenacious of life, and we shall find it by and by no small matter to keep them in check. Our native birds are much different, less prolific, less shrewd, less aggressive and persistent, less quick-witted and able to read the note of danger or hostility—in short, less sophisticated. Most of our birds are yet essentially wild, that is, little changed by civilization. In winter, especially, they sweep by me and around me in flocks,—the Canada sparrow, the snow-bunting, the shore-lark, the pine grosbeak, the red-poll, the cedar-bird,—feeding upon frozen apples in the orchard, upon cedar-berries, upon maple-buds, and the berries of the mountain ash, and the celtis, and upon the seeds of the weeds that rise above the snow in the field, or upon the hay-seed dropped where the cattle have been foddered in the barn-yard or about the distant stack; but yet taking no heed of man, in no way changing their habits so as to take advantage of his presence in nature. The pine grosbeak will come in numbers upon your porch, to get the black drupes of the honeysuckle or the woodbine, or within reach of your windows to get the berries of the mountain-ash, but they know you not; they look at you as innocently and unconcernedly as at a bear or moose in their native north, and your house is no more to them than a ledge of rocks.

The only ones of my winter neighbors that actually rap at my door are the nut-hatches and woodpeckers, and these do not know that it is my door. My retreat is covered with the bark of young chestnut-trees, and the birds, I suspect, mistake it for a huge stump that ought to hold fat grubs (there is not even a bookworm inside of it), and their loud rapping often makes me think I have a caller indeed. I place fragments of hickory-nuts in the interstices of the bark, and thus attract the nut-hatches; a bone upon my window-sill attracts both nut-hatches and the downy woodpecker. They peep in curiously through the window upon me, pecking away at my bone, too often a very poor one. A bone nailed to a tree a few feet in front of the window attracts crows as well as lesser birds. Even the slate-colored snow-bird, a seed-eater, comes and nibbles it occasionally.

The bird that seems to consider he has the best right to the bone both upon the tree and upon the sill is the downy woodpecker, my favorite neighbor among the winter

birds, to whom I will mainly devote the remainder of this
chapter. His retreat is but a few paces from my own, in the
decayed limb of an apple-tree which he excavated several
autumns ago. I say "he" because the red plume on the top
of his head proclaims the sex. It seems not to be generally
known to our writers upon ornithology that certain of our
woodpeckers—probably all the winter residents—each fall
excavate a limb or the trunk of a tree in which to pass the
winter, and that the cavity is abandoned in the spring,
probably for a new one in which nidification takes place.
So far as I have observed, these cavities are drilled out only
by the males. Where the females take up their quarters I
am not so well informed, though I suspect that they use
the abandoned holes of the males of the previous year.

The particular woodpecker to which I refer drilled his
first hole in my apple-tree one fall four or five years ago.
This he occupied till the following spring when he
abandoned it. The next fall he began a hole in an adjoining
limb, later than before, and when it was about half
completed a female took possession of his old quarters. I
am sorry to say that this seemed to enrage the male, very
much, and he persecuted the poor bird whenever she
appeared upon the scene. He would fly at her spitefully
and drive her off. One chilly November morning, as I
passed under the tree, I heard the hammer of the little
architect in his cavity, and at the same time saw the
persecuted female sitting at the entrance of the other hole
as if she would fain come out. She was actually shivering,
probably from both fear and cold. I understood the
situation at a glance; the bird was afraid to come forth and

brave the anger of the male. Not till I had rapped smartly upon the limb with my stick did she come out and attempt to escape; but she had not gone ten feet from the tree before the male was in hot pursuit, and in a few moments had driven her back to the same tree, where she tried to avoid him among the branches. A few days after, he rid himself of his unwelcome neighbor in the following ingenious manner: he fairly scuttled the other cavity; he drilled a hole into the bottom of it that let in the light and the cold, and I saw the female there no more. I did not see him in the act of rendering this tenement uninhabitable; but one morning, behold it was punctured at the bottom, and the circumstances all seemed to point to him as the author of it. There is probably no gallantry among the birds except at the mating season. I have frequently seen the male woodpecker drive the female away from the bone upon the tree. When she hopped around to the other end and timidly nibbled it, he would presently dart spitefully at her. She would then take up her position in his rear and wait till he had finished his meal. The position of the female among the birds is very much the same as that of woman among savage tribes. Most of the drudgery of life falls upon her, and the leavings of the males are often her lot.

My bird is a genuine little savage, doubtless, but I value him as a neighbor. It is a satisfaction during the cold or stormy winter nights to know he is warm and cosy there in his retreat. When the day is bad and unfit to be abroad in; he is there too. When I wish to know if he is at home, I go and rap upon his tree, and, if he is not too lazy or indifferent, after some delay he shows his head in his round doorway about ten feet above, and looks down inquiringly upon me—sometimes latterly I think half resentfully, as much as to say, "I would thank you not to disturb me so often." After sundown, he will not put his head out any more when I call, but as I step away I can get a glimpse of him inside looking cold and reserved. He is a late riser, especially if it is a cold or disagreeable morning, in this respect being like the fowls; it is sometimes near nine o'clock before I see him leave his tree. On the other hand, he comes home early, being in if the day is unpleasant by four P. M. He lives all alone; in this respect I do not commend his example. Where his mate is I should like to know.

I have discovered several other woodpeckers in adjoining orchards, each of which has a like home and leads a like solitary life. One of them has excavated a dry limb within easy reach of my hand, doing the work also in September. But the choice of tree was not a good one; the limb was too much decayed, and the workman had made the cavity too large; a chip had come out, making a hole in the outer wall. Then he went a few inches down the limb and began again, and excavated a large, commodious chamber, but had again come too near the surface; scarcely more than the bark protected him in one place, and the limb was very much weakened. Then he made another attempt still farther down the limb, and drilled in an inch or two, but seemed to change his mind; the work stopped, and I concluded the bird had wisely abandoned the tree. Passing there one cold, rainy November day, I thrust in my two fingers and was surprised to feel something soft and warm: as I drew away my hand the bird came out, apparently no more surprised than I was. It had decided, then, to make its home in the old limb; a decision it had occasion to regret, for not long after, on a stormy night, the branch gave way and fell to the ground.

When the bough breaks the cradle will fall,
and down will come baby, cradle and all.

Such a cavity makes a snug, warm home, and when the entrance is on the under side if the limb, as is usual, the wind and snow cannot reach the occupant. Late in December, while crossing a high, wooded mountain, lured by the music of fox-hounds, I discovered fresh yellow chips strewing the new-fallen snow, and at once thought of my woodpeckers. On looking around I saw where one had been at work excavating a lodge in a small yellow birch. The orifice was about fifteen feet from the ground, and appeared as round as if struck with a compass. It was on the east side of the tree, so as to avoid the prevailing west and northeast winds. As it was nearly two inches in diameter, it could not have been the work of the downy, but must have been that of the hairy, or else the yellow-bellied woodpecker. His home had probably been wrecked by some violent wind, and he was thus providing himself another. In digging out these retreats the woodpeckers prefer a dry, brittle, trunk, not too soft. They go in horizontally to the centre and then turn downward, enlarging the tunnel as they go, till when finished it is the shape of a long, deep pear.

Another trait our woodpeckers have that endears them to me, and that has never been pointedly noticed by our ornithologists, is their habit of drumming in the spring. They are songless birds, and yet all are musicians; they make the dry limbs eloquent of the coming change. Did you think that loud, sonorous hammering which proceeded from the orchard or from the near woods on that still March or April morning was only some bird getting its breakfast? It is downy, but he is not rapping at the door of a grub; he is rapping at the door of spring, and the dry limb thrills beneath the ardor of his blows. Or, later in the season, in the dense forest or by some remote mountain lake, does that measured rhythmic beat that breaks upon the silence, first three strokes following each other rapidly, succeeded by two louder ones with longer intervals between them, and that has an effect upon the alert ear as if the solitude itself had at last found a voice — does that suggest anything less than a deliberate musical performance? In fact, our woodpeckers are just as characteristically drummers as is the ruffed grouse, and they have their particular limbs and stubs to which they resort for that purpose. Their need of expression is apparently just as great as that of the song-birds, and it is not surprising that they should have found out that there is music in a dry, seasoned limb which can be evoked beneath their beaks.

A few seasons ago a downy woodpecker, probably the individual one who is now my winter neighbor, began to drum early in March in a partly decayed apple-tree that stands in the edge of a narrow strip of woodland near me. When the morning was still and mild I would often hear him through my window before I was up, or by half-past six o'clock, and he would keep it up pretty briskly till nine or ten o'clock, in this respect resembling the grouse, which do most of their drumming in the forenoon. His drum was the stub of a dry limb about the size of one's wrist. The heart was decayed and gone, but the outer shell was hard and resonant. The bird would keep his position there for an hour at a time. Between his drummings he would preen his plumage and listen as if for the response of the female, or for the drum of some rival. How swift his head would go when he was delivering his blows upon the limb! His beak wore the surface perceptibly. When he wished to change the key, which was quite often, he would shift his position an inch or two to a knot which gave out a higher, shriller note. When I climbed up to examine his drum he was much disturbed. I did not know he was in the vicinity, but it seems he saw me from a near tree, and came in haste to the neighboring branches, and with spread plumage and a sharp note demanded plainly enough what my business was with his drum. I was invading his privacy, desecrating his shrine, and the bird was much put out. After some weeks the female appeared; he had literally drummed up a mate; his urgent and oft-repeated advertisement was answered. Still the drumming did not cease, but was quite as fervent as before. If a mate could be won by drumming she could be kept and entertained by more drumming; courtship should not end with marriage. If the bird felt musical before, of course he felt much more so now. Besides that, the gentle deities needed propitiating in behalf of the nest and young as well as in behalf of the mate. After a time a second female came, when there was war between the two. I did not see them come to blows, but I saw one female pursuing the other about the place, and giving her no rest for several days. She was evidently trying to run her out of the neighborhood. Now and then she, too, would drum briefly as if sending a triumphant message to her mate.

The woodpeckers do not each have a particular dry limb to which they resort at all times to drum, like the one I have described. The woods are full of suitable branches, and they drum more or less here and there as they are in quest of food; yet I am convinced each one has its favorite spot, like the grouse, to which it resorts, especially in the morning. The sugar-maker in the maple-woods may notice that their sound proceeds from the same tree or trees about his camp with great regularity. A woodpecker in my vicinity has drummed for two seasons on a telegraph pole, and he makes the wires and glass insulators ring. Another drums on a thin board on the end of a long grape-arbor, and on still mornings can be heard a long distance.

A friend of mine in a Southern city tells me of a red-headed woodpecker that drums upon a lightning-rod on his neighbor's house. Nearly every clear, still morning at certain seasons, he says, this musical rapping may be heard. "He alternates his tapping with his stridulous call, and the effect on a cool, autumn-like morning is very pleasing."

The high-hole appears to drum more promiscuously than does the downy. He utters his long, loud spring call, whick—whick—whick—whick, and then begins to rap with his beak upon his perch before the last note has reached your ear. I have seen him drum sitting upon the ridge of the barn. The log cock, or pileated woodpecker, the largest and wildest of our Northern species, I have never heard drum. His blows should wake the echoes.

When the woodpecker is searching for food, or laying siege to some hidden grub, the sound of his hammer is dead or muffled, and is heard but a few yards. It is only upon dry, seasoned timber, freed of its bark, that he beats his reveille to spring and wooes his mate.

Wilson was evidently familiar with this vernal drumming of the woodpeckers, but quite misinterprets it. Speaking of the red-bellied species, he says: "It rattles like the rest of the tribe on the dead limbs, and with such violence as to be heard in still weather more than half a mile off; and listens to hear the insect it has alarmed." He listens rather to hear the drum of his rival or the brief and coy response of the female; for there are no insects in these dry limbs.

On one occasion I saw downy at his drum when a female flew quickly through the tree and alighted a few yards beyond him. He paused instantly, and kept his place, apparently without moving a muscle. The female, I took it, had answered his advertisement. She flitted about from limb to limb (the female may be known by the absence of the crimson spot on the back of the head), apparently full of business of her own, and now and then would drum in a shy, tentative manner. The male watched her a few moments and, convinced perhaps that she meant business, struck up his liveliest tune, then listened for her response. As it came back timidly but promptly, he left his perch and sought a nearer acquaintance with the prudent female. Whether or not a match grew out of this little flirtation I cannot say.

Our smaller woodpeckers are sometimes accused of injuring the apple and other fruit trees, but the depredator is probably the larger and rarer yellow-bellied species. One autumn I caught one of these fellows in the act of sinking long rows of his little wells in the limb of an apple-tree. There were series of rings of them, one above another, quite around the stem, some of them the third of an inch across. They are evidently made to get at the tender, juicy bark, or cambium layer, next to the hard wood of the tree. The health and vitality of the branch are so seriously impaired by them that it often dies.

In the following winter the same bird (probably) tapped a maple-tree in front of my window in fifty-six places; and when the day was sunny, and the sap oozed out, he spent most of his time there. He knew the good sap-days, and was on hand promptly for his tipple; cold and cloudy days he did not appear. He knew which side of the tree to tap, too, and avoided the sunless northern exposure. When one series of well-holes failed to supply him, he would sink another, drilling through the bark with great ease and quickness. Then, when the day was warm, and the sap ran freely, he would have a regular sugar-maple debauch, sitting there by his wells hour after hour, and as fast as they became filled sipping out the sap. This he did in a gentle, caressing manner that was very suggestive. He made a row of wells near the foot of the tree, and other rows higher up, and he would hop up and down the trunk as these became filled. He would hop down the tree backward with the utmost ease, throwing his tail outward and his head inward at each hop. When the wells would freeze or his thirst become slaked, he would ruffle his feathers, draw himself together, and sit and doze in the sun on the side of the tree. He passed the night in a hole in an apple-tree not far off. He was evidently a young bird not yet having the plumage of the mature male or female, and yet he knew which tree to tap and where to tap it. I saw where he had bored several maples in the vicinity, but no oaks or chestnuts. I nailed up a fat bone near his sap-works: the downy woodpecker came there several times a day to dine; the nut-hatch came, and even the snow-bird took a taste occasionally; but this sap-sucker never touched it; the sweet of the tree sufficed for him. This woodpecker does not breed or abound in my vicinity; only stray specimens are now and then to be met with in the colder months. As spring approached, the one I refer to took his departure.

I must bring my account of my neighbor in the tree down to the latest date; so after the lapse of a year I add the following notes. The last day of February was bright and springlike. I heard the first sparrow sing that morning and the first screaming of the circling hawks, and about seven o'clock the first drumming of my little friend. His first notes were uncertain and at long intervals, but by and by he warmed up and beat a lively tattoo. As the season advanced he ceased to lodge in his old quarters. I would rap and find nobody at home. Was he out on a lark, I said, the spring fever working in his blood? After a time his drumming grew less frequent, and finally, in the middle of April, ceased entirely. Had some accident befallen him, or had he wandered away to fresh fields, following some siren of his species? Probably the latter. Another bird that I had under observation also left his winter-quarters in the spring. This, then, appears to be the usual custom. The wrens and the nut-hatches and chickadees succeed to these abandoned cavities, and often have amusing disputes over them. The nut-hatches frequently pass the night in them, and the wrens and chickadees nest in them. I have further observed that in excavating a cavity for a nest the downy woodpecker makes the entrance smaller than when he is excavating his winter-quarters. This is doubtless for the greater safety of the young birds.

The next fall, the downy excavated another limb in the old apple-tree, but had not got his retreat quite finished, when the large hairy woodpecker appeared upon the scene. I heard his loud click, click, early one frosty November morning. There was something impatient and angry in the tone that arrested my attention. I saw the bird fly to the tree where downy had been at work, and fall with great violence upon the entrance to his cavity. The bark and the chips flew beneath his vigorous blows, and before I fairly woke up to what he was doing, he had completely demolished the neat, round doorway of downy. He had made a large ragged opening large enough for himself to enter. I drove him away and my favorite came back, but only to survey the ruins of his castle for a moment and then go away. He lingered about for a day or two and then disappeared. The big hairy usurper passed a night in the cavity, but on being hustled out of it the next night by me, he also left, but not till he had demolished the entrance to a cavity in a neighboring tree where downy and his mate had reared their brood that summer, and where I had hoped the female would pass the winter.

John Muir and John Burroughs.

April

If we represent the winter of our northern climate by a rugged snow-clad mountain, and summer by a broad fertile plain, then the intermediate belt, the hilly and breezy uplands, will stand for spring, with March reaching well up into the region of the snows, and April lapping well down upon the greening fields and unloosened currents, not beyond the limits of winter's sallying storms, but well within the vernal zone,—within the reach of the warm breath and subtle, quickening influences of the plain below. At its best, April is the tenderest of tender salads made crisp by ice or snow water. Its type is the first spear of grass. The senses—sight, hearing, smell—are as hungry for its delicate and almost spiritual tokens as the cattle are for the first bite of its fields. How it touches one and makes him both glad and sad! The voices of the arriving birds, the migrating fowls, the clouds of pigeons sweeping across the sky or filling the woods, the elfin horn of the first honeybee venturing abroad in the middle of the day, the clear piping of the little frogs in the marshes at sundown, the campfire in the sugar-bush, the smoke seen afar rising over the trees, the tinge of green that comes so suddenly on the sunny knolls and slopes, the full translucent streams, the waxing and warming sun,—how these things and others like them are noted by the eager eye and ear! April is my natal month, and I am born again into new delight and new surprises at each return of it. Its name has an indescribable charm to me. Its two syllables are like the calls of the first birds,—like that of the phoebe-bird, or of the meadowlark. Its very snows are fertilizing, and are called the poor man's manure.

Then its odors! I am thrilled by its fresh and indescribable odors,—the perfume of the bursting sod, of the quickened roots and rootlets, of the mould under the leaves, of the fresh furrows. No other month has odors like it. The west wind the other day came fraught with a perfume that was to the sense of smell what a wild and delicate strain of music is to the ear. It was almost transcendental. I walked across the hill with my nose in the air taking it in. It lasted for two days. I imagined it came from the willows of a distant swamp, whose catkins were affording the bees their first pollen: or did it come from much farther,—from beyond the horizon, the accumulated breath of innumerable farms and budding forests? The main characteristic of these April odors is their uncloying freshness. They are not sweet, they are oftener bitter, they are penetrating and lyrical. I know well the odors of May and June, of the world of meadows and orchards bursting into bloom, but they are not so ineffable and immaterial and so stimulating to the sense as the incense of April.

The season of which I speak does not correspond with the April of the almanac in all sections of our vast geography. It answers to March in Virginia and Maryland, while in parts of New York and New England it laps well over into May. It begins when the partridge drums, when the hyla pipes, when the shad start up the rivers, when the grass greens in the spring runs, and it ends when the leaves are unfolding and the last snowflake dissolves in midair. It may be the first of May before the first swallow appears, before the whip-poor-will is heard, before the wood thrush sings; but it is April as long as there is snow upon the mountains, no matter what the almanac may say. Our April is, in fact, a kind of Alpine summer, full of such contrasts and touches of wild, delicate beauty as no other season affords. The deluded citizen fancies there is nothing enjoyable in the country till June, and so misses the freshest, tenderest part. It is as if one should miss strawberries and begin his fruit-eating with melons and peaches. These last are good,—supremely so, they are melting and luscious,—but nothing so thrills and penetrates the taste, and wakes up and teases the papillae of the tongue, as the uncloying strawberry. What midsummer sweetness half so distracting as its brisk sub-acid flavor, and what splendor of full-leaved June can stir the blood like the best of leafless April?

One characteristic April feature, and one that delights me very much, is the perfect emerald of the spring runs while the fields are yet brown and sere,—strips and patches of the most vivid velvet green on the slopes and in the valleys. How the eye grazes there, and is filled and refreshed! I had forgotten what a marked feature this was until I recently rode in an open wagon for three days through a mountainous, pastoral country, remarkable for its fine springs. Those delicious green patches are yet in my eye. The fountains flowed with May. Where no springs occurred, there were hints and suggestions of springs about the fields and by the roadside in the freshened grass, —sometimes overflowing a space in the form of an actual fountain. The water did not quite get to the surface in such places, but sent its influence.

The fields of wheat and rye, too, how they stand out of the April landscape,—great green squares on a field of brown or gray!

Among April sounds there is none more welcome or suggestive to me than the voice of the little frogs piping in the marshes. No bird-note can surpass it as a spring token; and as it is not mentioned, to my knowledge, by the poets and writers of other lands, I am ready to believe it is characteristic of our season alone. You may be sure April has really come when this little amphibian creeps out of the mud and inflates its throat. We talk of the bird inflating its throat, but you should see this tiny minstrel inflate *its* throat, which becomes like a large bubble, and suggests a drummer-boy with his drum slung very high. In this drum, or by the aid of it, the sound is produced. Generally the note is very feeble at first, as if the frost was not yet all out of the creature's throat, and only one voice will be heard, some prophet bolder than all the rest, or upon whom the quickening ray of spring has first fallen. And it often happens that he is stoned for his pains by the yet unpacified element, and is compelled literally to "shut up" beneath a fall of snow or a heavy frost. Soon, however, he lifts up his voice again with more confidence, and is joined by others and still others, till in due time, say toward the last of the month, there is a shrill musical uproar, as the sun is setting, in every marsh and bog in the land. It is a plaintive sound, and I have heard people from the city speak of it as lonesome and depressing, but to the lover of the country it is a pure spring melody. The little piper will sometimes climb a bulrush, to which he clings like a sailor to a mast, and send forth his shrill call. There is a Southern species, heard when you have reached the Potomac, whose note is far more harsh and crackling. To stand on the verge of a swamp vocal with these, pains and stuns the ear. The call of the Northern species is far more tender and musical. [Footnote: The Southern species is called the green hyla. I have since heard them in my neighborhood on the Hudson.]

Then is there anything like a perfect April morning? One hardly knows what the sentiment of it is, but it is something very delicious. It is youth and hope. It is a new earth and a new sky. How the air transmits sounds, and what an awakening, prophetic character all sounds have! The distant barking of a dog, or the lowing of a cow, or the crowing of a cock, seems from out the heart of Nature, and to be a call to come forth. The great sun appears to have been reburnished, and there is something in his first glance above the eastern hills, and the way his eye-beams dart right and left and smite the rugged mountains into gold, that quickens the pulse and inspires the heart.

Across the fields in the early morning I hear some of the rare April birds,—the chewink and the brown thrasher. The robin, the bluebird, the song sparrow, the phoebe-bird, come in March; but these two ground-birds are seldom heard till toward the last of April. The ground-birds are all tree-singers or air-singers; they must have an elevated stage to speak from. Our long-tailed thrush, or thrasher, like its congeners the catbird and the mockingbird, delights in a high branch of some solitary tree, whence it will pour out its rich and intricate warble for an hour together. This bird is the great American chipper. There is no other bird that I know of that can chip with such emphasis and military decision as this yellow-eyed songster. It is like the click of a giant gunlock. Why is the thrasher so stealthy? It always seems to be going about on tiptoe. I never knew it to steal anything, and yet it skulks and hides like a fugitive from justice. One never sees it flying aloft in the air and traversing the world openly, like most birds, but it darts along fences and through bushes as if pursued by a guilty conscience. Only when the musical fit is upon it does it come up into full view, and invite the world to hear and behold.

The chewink is a shy bird also, but not stealthy. It is very inquisitive, and sets up a great scratching among the leaves, apparently to attract your attention. The male is perhaps the most conspicuously marked of all the ground-birds except the bobolink, being black above, bay on the sides, and white beneath. The bay is in compliment to the leaves he is forever scratching among,—they have rustled against his breast and sides so long that these parts have taken their color; but whence come the white and the black? The bird seems to be aware that his color betrays him, for there are few birds in the woods so careful about keeping themselves screened from view. When in song, its favorite perch is the top of some high bush near to cover. On being disturbed at such times, it pitches down into the brush and is instantly lost to view.

This is the bird that Thomas Jefferson wrote to Wilson about, greatly exciting the latter's curiosity. Wilson was just then upon the threshold of his career as an ornithologist, and had made a drawing of the Canada jay which he sent to the President. It was a new bird, and in reply Jefferson called his attention to a "curious bird" which was everywhere to be heard, but scarcely ever to be seen. He had for twenty years interested the young sportsmen of his neighborhood to shoot one for him, but without success. "It is in all the forests, from spring to fall," he says in his letter, "and never but on the tops of the tallest trees, from which it perpetually serenades us with some of the sweetest notes, and as clear as those of the nightingale. I have followed it for miles, without ever but once getting a good view of it. It is of the size and make of the mockingbird, lightly thrush-colored on the back, and a grayish white on the breast and belly. Mr. Randolph, my son-in-law, was in possession of one which had been shot by a neighbor," etc. Randolph pronounced it a flycatcher, which was a good way wide of the mark. Jefferson must have seen only the female, after all his tramp, from his description of the color; but he was doubtless following his own great thoughts more than the bird, else he would have had an earlier view. The bird was not a new one, but was well known then as the ground-robin. The President put Wilson on the wrong scent by his erroneous description, and it was a long time before the latter got at the truth of the case. But Jefferson's letter is a good sample of those which specialists often receive from intelligent persons who have seen or heard something in their line very curious or entirely new, and who set the man of science agog by a description of the supposed novelty,—a description that generally fits the facts of the case about as well as your coat fits the chair-back. Strange and curious things in the air, and in the water, and in the earth beneath, are seen every day except by those who are looking for them, namely, the naturalists. When Wilson or Audubon gets his eye on the unknown bird, the illusion vanishes, and your phenomenon turns out to be one of the commonplaces of the fields or woods.

A prominent April bird, that one does not have to go to the woods or away from his own door to see and hear, is the hardy and ever-welcome meadowlark. What a twang there is about this bird, and what vigor! It smacks of the soil. It is the winged embodiment of the spirit of our spring meadows. What emphasis in its *"z-d-t, z-d-t"* and what character in its long, piercing note! Its straight, tapering, sharp beak is typical of its voice. Its note goes like a shaft from a crossbow; it is a little too sharp and piercing when near at hand, but, heard in the proper perspective, it is eminently melodious and pleasing. It is one of the major notes of the fields at this season. In fact, it easily dominates all others. *"Spring o' the year! spring o' the year!"* it says, with a long-drawn breath, a little plaintive, but not complaining or melancholy. At times it indulges in something much more intricate and lark-like while hovering on the wing in midair, but a song is beyond the compass of its instrument, and the attempt usually ends in a breakdown. A clear, sweet, strong, high-keyed note, uttered from some knoll or rock, or stake in the fence, is its proper vocal performance. It has the build and walk and flight of the quail and the grouse. It gets up before you in much the same manner, and falls an easy prey to the crack shot. Its yellow breast, surmounted by a black crescent, it need not be ashamed to turn to the morning sun, while its coat of mottled gray is in perfect keeping with the stubble amid which it walks. The two lateral white quills in its tail seem strictly in character. These quills spring from a dash of scorn and defiance in the bird's make-up. By the aid of these, it can almost emit a flash as it struts about the fields and jerks out its sharp notes. They give a rayed, a definite and piquant expression to its movements. This bird is not properly a lark, but a starling, say the ornithologists, though it is lark-like in its habits, being a walker and entirely a ground-bird. Its color also allies it to the true lark. I believe there is no bird in the English or European fields that answers to this hardy pedestrian of our meadows. He is a true American, and his note one of our characteristic April sounds.

Another marked April note, proceeding sometimes from the meadows, but more frequently from the rough pastures and borders of the woods, is the call of the high-hole, or golden-shafted woodpecker. It is quite as strong as that of the meadowlark, but not so long-drawn and piercing. It is a succession of short notes rapidly uttered, as if the bird said *"if-if-if-if-if-if-if."* The notes of the ordinary downy and hairy woodpeckers suggest, in some way, the sound of a steel punch; but that of the high-hole is much softer, and strikes on the ear with real springtime melody. The high-hole is not so much a wood-pecker as he is a ground-pecker. He subsists largely on ants and crickets, and does not appear till they are to be found.

In Solomon's description of spring, the voice of the turtle is prominent, but our turtle, or mourning dove, though it arrives in April, can hardly be said to contribute noticeably to the open-air sounds. Its call is so vague, and soft, and mournful,—in fact, so remote and diffused,—that few persons ever hear it at all.

Such songsters as the cow blackbird are noticeable at this season, though they take a back seat a little later. It utters a peculiarly liquid April sound. Indeed, one would think its crop was full of water, its notes so bubble up and regurgitate, and are delivered with such an apparent stomachic contraction. This bird is the only feathered polygamist we have. The females are greatly in excess of the males, and the latter are usually attended by three or four of the former. As soon as the other birds begin to build, they are on the *qui vive*, prowling about like gypsies, not to steal the young of others, but to steal their eggs into other birds' nests, and so shirk the labor and responsibility of hatching and rearing their own young. As these birds do not mate, and as therefore there can be little or no rivalry or competition between the males, one wonders—in view of Darwin's teaching—why one sex should have brighter and richer plumage than the other, which is the fact. The males are easily distinguished from the dull and faded females by their deep glossy-black coats.

The April of English literature corresponds nearly to our May. In Great Britain, the swallow and the cuckoo usually arrive by the middle of April; with us, their appearance is a week or two later. Our April, at its best, is a bright, laughing face under a hood of snow, like the English March, but presenting sharper contrasts, a greater mixture of smiles and tears and icy looks than are known to our ancestral climate. Indeed, Winter sometimes retraces his steps in this month, and unburdens himself of the snows that the previous cold has kept back; but we are always sure of a number of radiant, equable days,—days that go before the bud, when the sun embraces the earth with fervor and determination. How his beams pour into the woods till the mould under the leaves is warm and emits an odor! The waters glint and sparkle, the birds gather in groups, and even those unused to singing find a voice. On the streets of the cities, what a flutter, what bright looks and gay colors! I recall one preëminent day of this kind last April. I made a note of it in my note-book. The earth seemed suddenly to emerge from a wilderness of clouds and chilliness into one of these blue sunlit spaces. How the voyagers rejoiced! Invalids came forth, old men sauntered down the street, stocks went up, and the political outlook brightened.

Such days bring out the last of the hibernating animals. The woodchuck unrolls and creeps out of his den to see if his clover has started yet. The torpidity leaves the snakes and the turtles, and they come forth and bask in the sun. There is nothing so small, nothing so great, that it does not respond to these celestial spring days, and give the pendulum of life a fresh start.

April is also the month of the new furrow. As soon as the frost is gone and the ground settled, the plow is started upon the hill, and at each bout I see its brightened mould-board flash in the sun. Where the last remnants of the snowdrift lingered yesterday the plow breaks the sod to-day. Where the drift was deepest the grass is pressed flat, and there is a deposit of sand and earth blown from the fields to windward. Line upon line the turf is reversed, until there stands out of the neutral landscape a ruddy square visible for miles, or until the breasts of the broad hills glow like the breasts of the robins.

Then who would not have a garden in April? to rake together the rubbish and burn it up, to turn over the renewed soil, to scatter the rich compost, to plant the first seed, or bury the first tuber! It is not the seed that is planted, any more than it is I that is planted; it is not the dry stalks and weeds that are burned up, any more than it is my gloom and regrets that are consumed. An April smoke makes a clean harvest.

I think April is the best month to be born in. One is just in time, so to speak, to catch the first train, which is made up in this month. My April chickens always turn out best. They get an early start; they have rugged constitutions. Late chickens cannot stand the heavy dews, or withstand the predaceous hawks. In April all nature starts with you. You have not come out of your hibernaculum too early or too late; the time is ripe, and, if you do not keep pace with the rest, why, the fault is not in the season.

Relaxing at Slabsides.

A Young Marsh Hawk

Most country boys, I fancy, know the marsh hawk. It is he you see flying low over the fields, beating about bushes and marshes and dip-ping over the fences, with his attention directed to the ground beneath him. He is a cat on wings. He keeps so low that the birds and mice do not see him till he is fairly upon them. The hen-hawk swoops down upon the meadow-mouse from his position high in air, or from the top of a dead tree; but the marsh hawk stalks him and comes suddenly upon him from over the fence, or from behind a low bush or tuft of grass. He is nearly as large as the hen-hawk, but has a much longer tail. When I was a boy, I used to call him the long-tailed hawk. The male is a bluish slate color; the female a reddish brown, like the hen-hawk, with a white rump.

Unlike the other hawks, they nest on the ground in low, thick marshy places. For several seasons a pair have nested in a bushy marsh a few miles back of me, near the house of a farmer friend of mine, who has a keen eye for the wild life about him. Two years ago he found the nest, but when I got over to see it the next week, it had been robbed, probably by some boys in the neighborhood - The past season, in April or May, by watching the mother bird, he found the nest again. It was in a marshy place, several acres in extent, in the bottom of a valley, and thickly grown with hardhack, prickly ash, smilax, and other low thorny bushes. My friend brought me to the brink of a low hill, and pointed out to me in the marsh below us, as nearly as he could, just where the nest was located. Then we crossed the pasture, entered upon the marsh, and made our way cautiously toward it. The wild thorny growths, waist high, had to be carefully dealt with. As we neared the spot, I used my eyes the best I could, but I did not see the hawk till she sprang into the air not ten yards away from us. She went screaming upward, and was soon sailing in a circle far above us. There, on a coarse matting of twigs and weeds, lay five snow-white eggs, a little more than half as large as hens' eggs. My companion said the male hawk would probably soon appear and join the female, but he did not. She kept drifting away to the east, and was soon gone from our sight.

We soon withdrew and secreted ourselves behind the stone wall, in hopes of seeing the mother hawk return. She appeared in the distance, but seemed to know she was being watched, and kept away. About ten days later we made another visit to the nest. An adventurous young Chicago lady also wanted to see a hawk's nest, and so accompanied us. This time three of the eggs were hatched, and as the mother hawk sprang up, either by accident or intentionally, she threw two of the young hawks some feet from the nest. She rose up and screamed angrily- Then, turning toward us, she came like an arrow straight at the young lady, a bright plume in whose hat probably drew her fire. The damsel gathered up her skirts about her and beat a hasty retreat. Hawks were not so pretty as she thought they were. A large hawk launched at one's face from high in the air is calculated to make one a little nervous. It is such a fearful incline down which the bird comes, and she is aiming exactly toward your eye. When within about thirty feet of you, she turns upward with a rushing sound, and, mounting higher, falls toward you again. She is only firing blank cartridges, as it were ; but it usually has the desired effect, and beats the enemy off.

After we had inspected the young hawks, a neighbor of my friend offered to conduct us to a quail's nest. Anything in the shape of a nest is always welcome, it is such a mystery, such a centre of interest and affection, and, if upon the ground, is usually something so dainty and exquisite amid the natural wreckage and confusion. A ground-nest seems so exposed, too, that it always gives a little thrill of pleasurable surprise to see the group of frail eggs resting there behind so slight a barrier. I will walk a long distance any day just to see a song sparrow's nest amid the stubble or under a tuft of grass. It is a jewel in a rosette of jewels, with a frill of weeds or turf. A quail's nest I had never seen, and to be shown one within the hunting-ground of this murderous hawk would be a double pleasure. Such a quiet, secluded, grass-grown highway as we moved along was itself a rare treat. Sequestered was the word that the little valley suggested, and peace the feeling the road evoked. The farmer, whose fields lay about us, half grown with weeds and bushes, evidently did not make stir or noise enough to disturb anything. Beside this rustic highway, bounded by old mossy stone walls, and within a stone's throw of the farmer's barn, the quail had made her nest. It was just under the edge of a prostrate thorn-bush.

"The nest is right there," said the farmer, pausing within ten feet of it, and pointing to the spot with his stick.

In a moment or two we could make out the mottled brown plumage of the sitting bird. Then we approached her cautiously till we bent above her.

She never moved a feather.

Then I put my cane down in the brush behind her. We wanted to see the eggs, yet did not want rudely to disturb the sitting hen.

She would not move.

Then I put down my hand within a few inches of her; still she kept her place. Should we have to lift her off bodily ?

Then the young lady put down her hand, probably the prettiest and the whitest hand the quail had ever seen. At least it started her, and off she sprang, uncovering such a crowded nest of eggs as I had never before beheld. Twenty-one of them! a ring or disk of white like a china tea-saucer. You could not help saying How pretty! How cunning! like baby hens' eggs, as if the bird were playing at sitting as children play at housekeeping.

If I had known how crowded her nest was, I should not have dared disturb her, for fear she would break some of them. But not an egg suffered harm by her sudden flight; and no harm came to the nest afterward. Every egg hatched, I was told, and the little chicks, hardly bigger than bumblebees, were led away by the mother into the fields.

In about a week I paid another visit to the hawk's nest. The eggs were all hatched, and the mother bird was hovering near. I shall never forget the curious expression of those young hawks sitting there on the ground. The expression was not one of youth, but of extreme age. Such an ancient, infirm look as they had, — the sharp, dark, and shrunken look about the face and eyes, and their feeble, tottering motions! They sat upon their elbows and the hind part of their bodies, and their pale, withered legs and feet extended before them in the most helpless fashion. Their angular bodies were covered with a pale yellowish down, like that of a chicken; their heads had a plucked, seedy appearance; and their long, strong, naked wings hung down by their sides till they touched the ground: power and ferocity in the first rude draught, shorn of everything but its sinister ugliness. Another curious thing was the gradation of the young in size; they tapered down regularly from the first to the fifth, as if there had been, as probably there was, an interval of a day or two between the hatchings.

The two older ones showed some signs of fear on our approach, and one of them threw himself upon his back, and put up his impotent legs, and glared at us with open beak. The two smaller ones regarded us not at all. Neither of the parent birds appeared during our stay.

When I visited the nest again, eight or ten days later, the birds were much grown, but of as marked a difference in size as before, and with the same look of extreme old age, — old age in men of the aquiline type, nose and chin coming together, and eyes large and sunken. They now glared upon us with a wild, savage look, and opened their beaks threateningly.

The next week, when my friend visited the nest, the larger of the hawks fought him savagely. But one of the brood, probably the last to hatch, had made but little growth. It appeared to be on the point of starvation. The mother hawk (for the male seemed to have disappeared) had perhaps found her family too large for her, and was deliberately allowing one of the number to perish; or did the larger and stronger young devour all the food before the weaker member could obtain any ? Probably this was the case.

Arthur brought the feeble nestling away, and the same day my little boy got it and brought it home, wrapped in a woolen rag. It was clearly a starved bantling. It cried feebly, but would not lift up its head.

We first poured some warm milk down its throat, which soon revived it, so that it would swallow small bits of flesh. In a day or two we had it eating ravenously, and its growth became noticeable. Its voice had the sharp whistling character of that of its parents, and was stilled only when the bird was asleep. We made a pen for it, about a yard square, in one end of the study, covering the floor with several thicknesses of newspapers; and here, upon a bit of brown woolen blanket for a nest, the hawk waxed strong day by day. An uglier-looking pet, tested by all the rules we usually apply to such things, would have been hard to find. There he would sit upon his elbows, his helpless feet out in front of him, his great featherless wings touching the floor, and shrilly cry for more food. For a time we gave him water daily from a stylograph-pen filler, but the water he evidently did not need or relish. Fresh meat, and plenty of it, was his demand. And we soon discovered that he liked game, such as mice, squirrels, birds, much better than butcher's meat.

Then began a lively campaign on the part of my little boy against all the vermin and small game in the neighborhood, to keep the hawk supplied. He trapped and he hunted, he enlisted his mates in his service, he even robbed the cats to feed the hawk. His usefulness as a boy of all work was seriously impaired. " Where is J ? " " Gone after a squirrel for his hawk." And often the day would be half gone before his hunt was successful. The premises were very soon cleared of mice, and the vicinity of chipmunks and squirrels. Farther and farther he was compelled to hunt the surrounding farms and woods to keep up with the demands of the hawk. By the time the hawk was ready to fly, he had consumed twenty-one chipmunks, fourteen red squirrels, sixteen mice, and twelve English sparrows, besides a lot of butcher's meat.

His plumage very soon began to show itself, crowding off tufts of the down. The quills on his great wings sprouted and grew apace. What a ragged, uncanny appearance he presented! but his look of extreme age gradually became modified. What a lover of the sunlight he was! We would put him out upon the grass, in the full blaze of the morning sun, and he would spread his wings and bask in it with the most intense enjoyment. In the nest the young must be exposed to the full power of the mid-day sun during our first heated terms in June and July, the thermometer often going up to ninety-three or ninety-five degrees, so that sunshine seemed to be a need of his nature. He liked the rain equally well, and when put out in a shower would sit down and take it as if every drop did him good.

His legs developed nearly as slowly as his wings. He could not stand steadily upon them till about ten days before he was ready to fly. The talons were limp and feeble. When we came with food, he would hobble along toward us like the worst kind of a cripple, drooping and moving his wings, and treading upon his legs from the foot back to the elbow, the foot remaining closed and useless. Like a baby learning to stand, he made many trials before he succeeded. He would rise up on his trembling legs only to fall back again.

One day, in the summer-house, I saw him for the first time stand for a moment squarely upon his legs with the feet fully spread beneath them. He looked about him as if the world suddenly wore a new aspect.

His plumage now grew quite rapidly. One red squirrel a day, chopped fine with an axe, was his > ration. He began to hold his game with his foot while he tore it.

The study was full of his shed down. His dark brown mottled plumage began to grow beautiful. The wings drooped a little, but gradually he got control of them, and held them in place.

It was now the 20th of July, and the hawk was about five weeks old. In a day or two he was walking or jumping about the ground. He chose a position under the edge of a Norway spruce, where he would sit for hours dozing, or looking out upon the landscape. When we brought him game, he would advance to meet us with wings slightly lifted, and uttering a shrill cry. Toss him a mouse or sparrow, and he would seize it with one foot and hop off to his cover, where he would bend above it, spread his plumage, look this way and that, uttering all the time the most exultant and satisfied chuckle.

About this time he began to practice striking with his talons, as an Indian boy might begin practicing with his bow and arrow. He would strike at a dry leaf in the grass, or at a fallen apple, or at some imaginary object. He was learning the use of his weapons. His wings also, — he seemed to feel them sprouting from his shoulders. He would lift them straight up and hold them expanded, and they would seem to quiver with excitement. Every hour in the day he would do this. The pressure was beginning to centre there. Then he would strike playfully at a leaf or a bit of wood, and keep his wings lifted.

The next step was to spring into the air and beat his wings. He seemed now to be thinking entirely of his wings. They itched to be put to use.

A day or two later he would leap and fly several feet. A pile of brush ten or twelve feet below the bank was easily reached. Here he would perch in true hawk fashion, to the bewilderment and scandal of all the robins and catbirds in the vicinity. Here he would dart his eye in all directions, turning his head over and glancing up into the sky.

He was now a lovely creature, fully fledged, and as tame as a kitten. But he was not a bit like a kitten in one respect, — he could not bear to have you stroke or even touch his plumage. He had a horror of your hand, as if it would hopelessly defile him. But he would perch upon it, and allow you to carry him about. If a dog or cat appeared, he was ready to give battle instantly. He rushed up to a little dog one day, and struck him with his foot savagely. He was afraid of strangers, and of any unusual object.

The last week in July he began to fly quite freely, and it was necessary to clip one of his wings. As the clipping embraced only the ends of his primaries, he soon overcame the difficulty, and by carrying his broad, long tail more on that side, flew with considerable ease. He made longer and longer excursions into the surrounding fields and vineyards, and did not always return. On such occasions we would go find him and fetch him back.

Late one rainy afternoon he flew away into the vineyard, and when, an hour later, I went after him, he could not be found, and we never saw him again. We hoped hunger would soon drive him back, but we have had no clew to him from that day to this.

Strawberries

Was it old Dr. Parr who said or sighed in his last illness, "Oh, if I can only live till strawberries come!" The old scholar imagined that, if he could weather it till then, the berries would carry him through. No doubt he had turned from the drugs and the nostrums, or from the hateful food, to the memory of the pungent, penetrating, and unspeakably fresh quality of the strawberry with the deepest longing. The very thought of these crimson lobes, embodying as it were the first glow and ardor of the young summer, and with their power to unsheathe the taste and spur the nagging appetite, made life seem possible and desirable to him.

The strawberry is always the hope of the invalid, and sometimes, no doubt, his salvation. It is the first and finest relish among fruits, and well merits Dr. Boteler's memorable saying, that "doubtless God could have made a better berry, but doubtless God never did."

On the threshold of summer, Nature proffers us this her virgin fruit; more rich and sumptuous are to follow, but the wild delicacy and fillip of the strawberry are never repeated,—that keen feathered edge greets the tongue in nothing else.

Let me not be afraid of overpraising it, but probe and probe for words to hint its surprising virtues. We may well celebrate it with festivals and music. It has that indescribable quality of all first things,—that shy, uncloying, provoking barbed sweetness. It is eager and sanguine as youth. It is born of the copious dews, the fragrant nights, the tender skies, the plentiful rains of the early season. The singing of birds is in it, and the health and frolic of lusty Nature. It is the product of liquid May touched by the June sun. It has the tartness, the briskness, the unruliness of spring, and the aroma and intensity of summer.

Oh, the strawberry days! how vividly they come back to one! The smell of clover in the fields, of blooming rye on the hills, of the wild grape beside the woods, and of the sweet honeysuckle and the spiræa about the house. The first hot, moist days. The daisies and the buttercups; the songs of the birds, their first reckless jollity and love-making over; the full tender foliage of the trees; the bees swarming, and the air strung with resonant musical chords. The time of the sweetest and most, succulent grass, when the cows come home with aching udders. Indeed, the strawberry belongs to the juiciest time of the year.

What a challenge it is to the taste! how it bites back again! and is there any other sound like the snap and crackle with which it salutes the ear on being plucked from the stems? It is a threat to one sense that the other is soon to verify. It snaps to the ear as it smacks to the tongue. All other berries are tame beside it.

The plant is almost an evergreen; it loves the coverlid of the snow, and will keep fresh through the severest winters with a slight protection. The frost leaves its virtues in it. The berry is a kind of vegetable snow. How cool, how tonic, how melting, and how perishable! It is almost as easy to keep frost. Heat kills it, and sugar quickly breaks up its cells.

Is there anything like the odor of strawberries? The next best thing to tasting them is to smell them; one may put his nose to the dish while the fruit is yet too rare and choice for his fingers. Touch not and taste not, but take a good smell and go mad! Last fall I potted some of the Downer, and in the winter grew them in the house. In March the berries were ripe, only four or five on a plant, just enough, all told, to make one consider whether it were not worth while to kill off the rest of the household, so that the berries need not be divided. But if every tongue could not have a feast, every nose banqueted daily upon them. They filled the house with perfume. The Downer is remarkable in this respect. Grown in the open field, it surpasses in its odor any strawberry of my acquaintance. And it is scarcely less agreeable to the taste. It is a very beautiful berry to look upon, round, light pink, with a delicate, fine-grained expression. Some berries shine, the Downer glows as if there were a red bloom upon it. Its core is firm and white, its skin thick and easily bruised, which makes it a poor market berry, but, with its high flavor and productiveness, an admirable one for home use. It seems to be as easily grown as the Wilson, while it is much more palatable. The great trouble with the Wilson, as everybody knows, is its rank acidity. When it first comes, it is difficult to eat it without making faces. It is crabbed and acrimonious. Like some persons, the Wilson will not ripen and sweeten till its old age. Its largest and finest crop, if allowed to remain on the vines, will soften and fail unregenerated, or with all its sins upon it. But wait till toward the end of the season, after the plant gets over its hurry and takes time to ripen its fruit. The berry will then face the sun for days, and, if the weather is not too wet, instead of softening will turn dark and grow rich. Out of its crabbedness and spitefulness come the finest, choicest flavors. It is an astonishing berry. It lays hold of the taste in a way that the aristocratic berries, like the Jocunda or the Triumph, cannot approximate to. Its quality is as penetrating as that of ants and wasps, but sweet. It is, indeed, a wild bee turned into a berry, with the sting mollified and the honey disguised. A quart of these rare-ripes I venture to say contains more of the peculiar virtue and excellence of the strawberry kind than can be had in twice the same quantity of any other cultivated variety. Take these berries in a bowl of rich milk with some bread, —ah, what a dish!—too good to set before a king! I suspect this was the food of Adam in Paradise, only Adam did not have the Wilson strawberry; he had the wild strawberry that Eve plucked in their hill-meadow and "hulled" with her own hands, and that, take it all in all, even surpasses the late-ripened Wilson.

Adam is still extant in the taste and the appetite of most country boys; lives there a country boy who does not like wild strawberries and milk,—yea, prefer it to any other known dish? I am not thinking of a dessert of strawberries and cream; this the city boy may have, too, after a sort; but bread-and-milk, with the addition of wild strawberries, is peculiarly a country dish, and is to the taste what a wild bird's song is to the ear. When I was a lad, and went afield with my hoe or with the cows, during the strawberry season, I was sure to return at meal-time with a lining of berries in the top of my straw hat. They were my daily food, and I could taste the liquid and gurgling notes of the bobolink in every spoonful of them; and to this day, to make a dinner or supper off a bowl of milk with bread and strawberries, — plenty of strawberries, — well, is as near to being a boy again as I ever expect to come. The golden age draws sensibly near. Appetite becomes a kind of delicious thirst, — a gentle and subtle craving of all parts of the mouth and throat, — and those nerves of taste that occupy, as it were, a back seat, and take little cognizance of grosser foods, come forth, and are played upon and set vibrating. Indeed, I think, if there is ever rejoicing throughout one's alimentary household, — if ever that much-abused servant, the stomach, says Amen, or those faithful handmaidens, the liver and spleen, nudge each other delightedly, it must be when one on a torrid summer day passes by the solid and carnal dinner for this simple Arcadian dish.

The wild strawberry, like the wild apple, is spicy and high-flavored, but, unlike the apple, it is also mild and delicious. It has the true rustic sweetness and piquancy. What it lacks in size, when compared with the garden berry, it makes up in intensity. It is never dropsical or overgrown, but firm-fleshed and hardy. Its great enemies are the plow, gypsum, and the horse-rake. It dislikes a limestone soil, but seems to prefer the detritus of the stratified rock. Where the sugar maple abounds, I have always found plenty of wild strawberries. We have two kinds,—the wood berry and the field berry. The former is as wild as a partridge. It is found in open places in the woods and along the borders, growing beside stumps and rocks, never in abundance, but very sparsely. It is small, cone-shaped, dark red, shiny, and pimply. It looks woody, and tastes so. It has never reached the table, nor made the acquaintance of cream. A quart of them, at a fair price for human labor, would be worth their weight in silver at least. (Yet a careful observer writes me that in certain sections in the western part of New York they are very plentiful.)

Ovid mentions the wood strawberry, which would lead one to infer that they were more abundant in his time and country than in ours.

This is, perhaps, the same as the alpine strawberry, which is said to grow in the mountains of Greece, and thence northward. This was probably the first variety cultivated, though our native species would seem as unpromising a subject for the garden as club-moss or wintergreens.

Of the field strawberry there are a great many varieties,—some growing in meadows, some in pastures, and some upon mountain-tops. Some are round, and stick close to the calyx or hull; some are long and pointed, with long, tapering necks. These usually grow upon tall stems. They are, indeed, of the slim, linear kind. Your corpulent berry keeps close to the ground; its stem and foot-stalk are short, and neck it has none. Its color is deeper than that of its tall brother, and of course it has more juice. You are more apt to find the tall varieties upon knolls in low, wet meadows, and again upon mountain-tops, growing in tussocks of wild grass about the open summits. These latter ripen in July, and give one his last taste of strawberries for the season.

But the favorite haunt of the wild strawberry is an uplying meadow that has been exempt from the plow for five or six years, and that has little timothy and much daisy. When you go a-berrying, turn your steps toward the milk-white meadows. The slightly bitter odor of the daisies is very agreeable to the smell, and affords a good background for the perfume of the fruit. The strawberry cannot cope with the rank and deep-rooted clover, and seldom appears in a field till the clover has had its day. But the daisy with its slender stalk does not crowd or obstruct the plant, while its broad white flower is like a light parasol that tempers and softens the too strong sunlight. Indeed, daisies and strawberries are generally associated. Nature fills her dish with the berries, then covers them with the white and yellow of milk and cream, thus suggesting a combination we are quick to follow. Milk alone, after it loses its animal heat, is a clod, and begets torpidity of the brain; the berries lighten it, give wings to it, and one is fed as by the air he breathes or the water he drinks.

Then the delight of "picking" the wild berries! It is one of the fragrant memories of boyhood. Indeed, for boy or man to go a-berrying in a certain pastoral country I know of, where a passer-by along the highway is often regaled by a breeze loaded with a perfume of the o'er-ripe fruit, is to get nearer to June than by almost any course I know of. Your errand is so private and confidential! You stoop low. You part away the grass and the daisies, and would lay bare the inmost secrets of the meadow. Everything is yet tender and succulent; the very air is bright and new; the warm breath of the meadow comes up in your face; to your knees you are in a sea of daisies and clover; from your knees up, you are in a sea of solar light and warmth. Now you are prostrate like a swimmer, or like a surf-bather reaching for pebbles or shells, the white and green spray breaks above you; then, like a devotee before a shrine or naming his beads, your rosary strung with luscious berries; anon you are a grazing Nebuchadnezzar, or an artist taking an inverted view of the landscape.

The birds are alarmed by your close scrutiny of their domain. They hardly know whether to sing or to cry, and do a little of both. The bobolink follows you and circles above and in advance of you, and is ready to give you a triumphal exit from the field, if you will only depart.

Ye boys that gather flowers and strawberries,
Lo, hid within the grass, an adder lies,

Warton makes Virgil sing; and Montaigne, in his "Journey to Italy," says: "The children very often are afraid, on account of the snakes, to go and pick the strawberries that grow in quantities on the mountains and among bushes." But there is no serpent here,—at worst, only a bumblebee's or yellow-jacket's nest. You soon find out the spring in the corner of the field under the beechen tree. While you wipe your brow and thank the Lord for spring water, you glance at the initials in the bark, some of them so old that they seem runic and legendary. You find out, also, how gregarious the strawberry is,—that the different varieties exist in little colonies about the field. When you strike the outskirts of one of these plantations, how quickly you work toward the centre of it, and then from the centre out, then circumnavigate it, and follow up all its branchings and windings!

Then the delight in the abstract and in the concrete of strolling and lounging about the June meadows; of lying in pickle for half a day or more in this pastoral sea, laved by the great tide, shone upon by the virile sun, drenched to the very marrow of your being with the warm and wooing influences of the young summer!

I was a famous berry-picker when a boy. It was near enough to hunting and fishing to enlist me. Mother would always send me in preference to any of the rest of the boys. I got the biggest berries and the most of them. There was something of the excitement of the chase in the occupation, and something of the charm and preciousness of game about the trophies. The pursuit had its surprises, its expectancies, its sudden disclosures,—in fact, its uncertainties. I went forth adventurously. I could wander free as the wind. Then there were moments of inspiration, for it always seemed a felicitous stroke to light upon a particularly fine spot, as it does when one takes an old and wary trout. You discovered the game where it was hidden. Your genius prompted you. Another had passed that way and had missed the prize. Indeed, the successful berry-picker, like Walton's angler, is born, not made. It is only another kind of angling. In the same field one boy gets big berries and plenty of them; another wanders up and down, and finds only a few little ones. He cannot see them; he does not know how to divine them where they lurk under the leaves and vines. The berry-grower knows that in the cultivated patch his pickers are very unequal, the baskets of one boy or girl having so inferior a look that it does not seem possible they could have been filled from the same vines with certain others. But neither blunt fingers nor blunt eyes are hard to find; and as there are those who can see nothing clearly, so there are those who can touch nothing deftly or gently.

The cultivation of the strawberry is thought to be comparatively modern. The ancients appear to have been a carnivorous race: they gorged themselves with meat; while the modern man makes larger and larger use of fruits and vegetables, until this generation is doubtless better fed than any that has preceded it. The strawberry and the apple, and such vegetables as celery, ought to lengthen human life,—at least to correct its biliousness and make it more sweet and sanguine.

The first impetus to strawberry culture seems to have been given by the introduction of our field berry (*Fragaria Virginiana*) into England in the seventeenth century, though not much progress was made till the eighteenth. This variety is much more fragrant and aromatic than the native berry of Europe, though less so in that climate than when grown here. Many new seedlings sprang from it, and it was the prevailing berry in English and French gardens, says Fuller, until the South American species, *grandiflora*, was introduced and supplanted it. This berry is naturally much larger and sweeter, and better adapted to the English climate, than our *Virginiana*. Hence the English strawberries of to-day surpass ours in these respects, but are wanting in that aromatic pungency that characterizes most of our berries.

The Jocunda, Triumph, Victoria, are foreign varieties of the Grandiflora species; while the Hovey, the Boston Pine, the Downer, are natives of this country.

The strawberry, in the main, repeats the form of the human heart, and perhaps, of all the small fruits known to man, none other is so deeply and fondly cherished, or hailed with such universal delight, as this lowly but youth-renewing berry.

Speckled Trout

The legend of the wary trout, hinted at in the last sketch, is to be further illustrated in this and some following chapters. We shall get at more of the meaning of those dark water-lines, and I hope, also, not entirely miss the significance of the gold and silver spots and the glancing iridescent hues. The trout is dark and obscure above, but behind this foil there are wondrous tints that reward the believing eye. Those who seek him in his wild remote haunts are quite sure to get the full force of the sombre and uninviting aspects,—the wet, the cold, the toil, the broken rest, and the huge, savage, uncompromising nature,—but the true angler sees farther than these, and is never thwarted of his legitimate reward by them.

I have been a seeker of trout from my boyhood, and on all the expeditions in which this fish has been the ostensible purpose I have brought home more game than my creel showed. In fact, in my mature years I find I got more of nature into me, more of the woods, the wild, nearer to bird and beast, while threading my native streams for trout, than in almost any other way. It furnished a good excuse to go forth; it pitched one in the right key; it sent one through the fat and marrowy places of field and wood. Then the fisherman has a harmless, preoccupied look; he is a kind of vagrant that nothing fears. He blends himself with the trees and the shadows.

All his approaches are gentle and indirect. He times himself to the meandering, soliloquizing stream; its impulse bears him along. At the foot of the waterfall he sits sequestered and hidden in its volume of sound. The birds know he has no designs upon them, and the animals see that his mind is in the creek. His enthusiasm anneals him, and makes him pliable to the scenes and influences he moves among.

Then what acquaintance he makes with the stream! He addresses himself to it as a lover to his mistress; he wooes it and stays with it till he knows its most hidden secrets. It runs through his thoughts not less than through its banks there; he feels the fret and thrust of every bar and boulder. Where it deepens, his purpose deepens; where it is shallow, he is indifferent. He knows how to interpret its every glance and dimple; its beauty haunts him for days.

I am sure I run no risk of overpraising the charm and attractiveness of a well-fed trout stream, every drop of water in it as bright and pure as if the nymphs had brought it all the way from its source in crystal goblets, and as cool as if it had been hatched beneath a glacier. When the heated and soiled and jaded refugee from the city first sees one, he feels as if he would like to turn it into his bosom and let it flow through him a few hours, it suggests such healing freshness and newness. How his roily thoughts would run clear; how the sediment would go downstream! Could he ever have an impure or an unwholesome wish afterward? The next best thing he can do is to tramp along its banks and surrender himself to its influence. If he reads it intently enough, he will, in a measure, be taking it into his mind and heart, and experiencing its salutary ministrations.

Trout streams coursed through every valley my boyhood knew. I crossed them, and was often lured and detained by them, on my way to and from school. We bathed in them during the long summer noons, and felt for the trout under their banks. A holiday was a holiday indeed that brought permission to go fishing over on Rose's Brook, or up Hardscrabble, or in Meeker's Hollow; all-day trips, from morning till night, through meadows and pastures and beechen woods, wherever the shy, limpid stream led. What an appetite it developed! a hunger that was fierce and aboriginal, and that the wild strawberries we plucked as we crossed the hill teased rather than allayed. When but a few hours could be had, gained perhaps by doing some piece of work about the farm or garden in half the allotted time, the little creek that headed in the paternal domain was handy; when half a day was at one's disposal, there were the hemlocks, less than a mile distant, with their loitering, meditative, log-impeded stream and their dusky, fragrant depths. Alert and wide-eyed, one picked his way along, startled now and then by the sudden bursting-up of the partridge, or by the whistling wings of the "dropping snipe," pressing through the brush and the briers, or finding an easy passage over the trunk of a prostrate tree, carefully letting his hook down through some tangle into a still pool, or standing in some high, sombre avenue and watching his line float in and out amid the moss-covered boulders. In my first essayings I used to go to the edge of these hemlocks, seldom dipping into them beyond the first pool where the stream swept under the roots of two large trees. From this point I could look back into the sunlit fields where the cattle were grazing; beyond, all was gloom and mystery; the trout were black, and to my young imagination the silence and the shadows were blacker. But gradually I yielded to the fascination and penetrated the woods farther and farther on each expedition, till the heart of the mystery was fairly plucked out. During the second or third year of my piscatorial experience I went through them, and through the pasture and meadow beyond, and through another strip of hemlocks, to where the little stream joined the main creek of the valley.

In June, when my trout fever ran pretty high, and an auspicious day arrived, I would make a trip to a stream a couple of miles distant, that came down out of a comparatively new settlement. It was a rapid mountain brook presenting many difficult problems to the young angler, but a very enticing stream for all that, with its two saw-mill dams, its pretty cascades, its high, shelving rocks sheltering the mossy nests of the phœbe-bird, and its general wild and forbidding aspects.

But a meadow brook was always a favorite. The trout like meadows; doubtless their food is more abundant there, and, usually, the good hiding-places are more numerous. As soon as you strike a meadow the character of the creek changes: it goes slower and lies deeper; it tarries to enjoy the high, cool banks and to half hide beneath them; it loves the willows, or rather the willows love it and shelter it from the sun; its spring runs are kept cool by the overhanging grass, and the heavy turf that faces its open banks is not cut away by the sharp hoofs of the grazing cattle. Then there are the bobolinks and the starlings and the meadowlarks, always interested spectators of the angler; there are also the marsh marigolds, the buttercups, or the spotted lilies, and the good angler is always an interested spectator of them. In fact, the patches of meadow land that lie in the angler's course are like the happy experiences in his own life, or like the fine passages in the poem he is reading; the pasture oftener contains the shallow and monotonous places. In the small streams the cattle scare the fish, and soil their element and break down their retreats under the banks. Woodland alternates the best with meadow: the creek loves to burrow under the roots of a great tree, to scoop out a pool after leaping over the prostrate trunk of one, and to pause at the foot of a ledge of moss-covered rocks, with ice-cold water dripping down. How straight the current goes for the rock! Note its corrugated, muscular appearance; it strikes and glances off, but accumulates, deepens with well-defined eddies above and to one side; on the edge of these the trout lurk and spring upon their prey.

The angler learns that it is generally some obstacle or hindrance that makes a deep place in the creek, as in a brave life; and his ideal brook is one that lies in deep, well-defined banks, yet makes many a shift from right to left, meets with many rebuffs and adventures, hurled back upon itself by rocks, waylaid by snags and trees, tripped up by precipices, but sooner or later reposing under meadow banks, deepening and eddying beneath bridges, or prosperous and strong in some level stretch of cultivated land with great elms shading it here and there.

But I early learned that from almost any stream in a trout country the true angler could take trout, and that the great secret was this, that, whatever bait you used, worm, grasshopper, grub, or fly, there was one thing you must always put upon your hook, namely, your heart: when you bait your hook with your heart the fish always bite; they will jump clear from the water after it; they will dispute with each other over it; it is a morsel they love above everything else. With such bait I have seen the born angler (my grandfather was one) take a noble string of trout from the most unpromising waters, and on the most unpromising day. He used his hook so coyly and tenderly, he approached the fish with such address and insinuation, he divined the exact spot where they lay: if they were not eager, he humored them and seemed to steal by them; if they were playful and coquettish, he would suit his mood to theirs; if they were frank and sincere, he met them halfway; he was so patient and considerate, so entirely devoted to pleasing the critical trout, and so successful in his efforts,—surely his heart was upon his hook, and it was a tender, unctuous heart, too, as that of every angler is. How nicely he would measure the distance! how dexterously he would avoid an overhanging limb or bush and drop the line exactly in the right spot! Of course there was a pulse of feeling and sympathy to the extremity of that line. If your heart is a stone, however, or an empty husk, there is no use to put it upon your hook; it will not tempt the fish; the bait must be quick and fresh. Indeed, a certain quality of youth is indispensable to the successful angler, a certain unworldliness and readiness to invest yourself in an enterprise that doesn't pay in the current coin. Not only is the angler, like the poet, born and not made, as Walton says, but there is a deal of the poet in him, and he is to be judged no more harshly; he is the victim of his genius: those wild streams, how they haunt him! he will play truant to dull care, and flee to them; their waters impart somewhat of their own perpetual youth to him. My grandfather when he was eighty years old would take down his pole as eagerly as any boy, and step off with wonderful elasticity toward the beloved streams; it used to try my young legs a good deal to follow him, specially on the return trip. And no poet was ever more innocent of worldly success or ambition. For, to paraphrase Tennyson,

Lusty trout to him were scrip and share,
And babbling waters more than cent for cent.

He laid up treasures, but they were not in this world. In fact, though the kindest of husbands, I fear he was not what the country people call a "good provider," except in providing trout in their season, though it is doubtful if there was always fat in the house to fry them in. But he could tell you they were worse off than that at Valley Forge, and that trout, or any other fish, were good roasted in the ashes under the coals. He had the Walton requisite of loving quietness and contemplation, and was devout withal. Indeed, in many ways he was akin to those Galilee fishermen who were called to be fishers of men. How he read the Book and pored over it, even at times, I suspect, nodding over it, and laying it down only to take up his rod, over which, unless the trout were very dilatory and the journey very fatiguing, he never nodded!

II

The Delaware is one of our minor rivers, but it is a stream beloved of the trout. Nearly all its remote branches head in mountain springs, and its collected waters, even when warmed by the summer sun, are as sweet and wholesome as dew swept from the grass. The Hudson wins from it two streams that are fathered by the mountains from whose loins most of its beginnings issue, namely, the Rondout and the Esopus. These swell a more illustrious current than the Delaware, but the Rondout, one of the finest trout streams in the world, makes an uncanny alliance before it reaches its destination, namely, with the malarious Wallkill.

In the same nest of mountains from which they start are born the Neversink and the Beaverkill, streams of wondrous beauty that flow south and west into the Delaware. From my native hills I could catch glimpses of the mountains in whose laps these creeks were cradled, but it was not till after many years, and after dwelling in a country where trout are not found, that I returned to pay my respects to them as an angler.

My first acquaintance with the Neversink was made in company with some friends in 1869. We passed up the valley of the Big Ingin, marveling at its copious ice-cold springs, and its immense sweep of heavy-timbered mountain-sides. Crossing the range at its head, we struck the Neversink quite unexpectedly about the middle of the afternoon, at a point where it was a good-sized trout stream. It proved to be one of those black mountain brooks born of innumerable ice-cold springs, nourished in the shade, and shod, as it were, with thick-matted moss, that every camper-out remembers. The fish are as black as the stream and very wild. They dart from beneath the fringed rocks, or dive with the hook into the dusky depths,—an integral part of the silence and the shadows. The spell of the moss is over all. The fisherman's tread is noiseless, as he leaps from stone to stone and from ledge to ledge along the bed of the stream. How cool it is! He looks up the dark, silent defile, hears the solitary voice of the water, sees the decayed trunks of fallen trees bridging the stream, and all he has dreamed, when a boy, of the haunts of beasts of prey—the crouching feline tribes, especially if it be near nightfall and the gloom already deepening in the woods— comes freshly to mind, and he presses on, wary and alert, and speaking to his companions in low tones.

After an hour or so the trout became less abundant, and with nearly a hundred of the black sprites in our baskets we turned back. Here and there I saw the abandoned nests of the pigeons, sometimes half a dozen in one tree. In a yellow birch which the floods had uprooted, a number of nests were still in place, little shelves or platforms of twigs loosely arranged, and affording little or no protection to the eggs or the young birds against inclement weather.

Before we had reached our companions the rain set in again and forced us to take shelter under a balsam. When it slackened we moved on and soon came up with Aaron, who had caught his first trout, and, considerably drenched, was making his way toward camp, which one of the party had gone forward to build. After traveling less than a mile, we saw a smoke struggling up through the dripping trees, and in a few moments were all standing round a blazing fire. But the rain now commenced again, and fairly poured down through the trees, rendering the prospect of cooking and eating our supper there in the woods, and of passing the night on the ground without tent or cover of any kind, rather disheartening. We had been told of a bark shanty a couple of miles farther down the creek, and thitherward we speedily took up our line of march. When we were on the point of discontinuing the search, thinking we had been misinformed or had passed it by, we came in sight of a bark-peeling, in the midst of which a small log house lifted its naked rafters toward the now breaking sky. It had neither floor nor roof, and was less inviting on first sight than the open woods. But a board partition was still standing, out of which we built a rude porch on the east side of the house, large enough for us all to sleep under if well packed, and eat under if we stood up. There was plenty of well-seasoned timber lying about, and a fire was soon burning in front of our quarters that made the scene social and picturesque, especially when the frying-pans were brought into requisition, and the coffee, in charge of Aaron, who was an artist in this line, mingled its aroma with the wild-wood air. At dusk a balsam was felled, and the tips of the branches used to make a bed, which was more fragrant than soft; hemlock is better, because its needles are finer and its branches more elastic.

There was a spirt or two of rain during the night, but not enough to find out the leaks in our roof. It took the shower or series of showers of the next day to do that. They commenced about two o'clock in the afternoon. The forenoon had been fine, and we had brought into camp nearly three hundred trout; but before they were half dressed, or the first panfuls fried, the rain set in. First came short, sharp dashes, then a gleam of treacherous sunshine, followed by more and heavier dashes. The wind was in the southwest, and to rain seemed the easiest thing in the world. From fitful dashes to a steady pour the transition was natural. We stood huddled together, stark and grim, under our cover, like hens under a cart. The fire fought bravely for a time, and retaliated with sparks and spiteful tongues of flame; but gradually its spirit was broken, only a heavy body of coal and half-consumed logs in the centre holding out against all odds. The simmering fish were soon floating about in a yellow liquid that did not look in the least appetizing. Point after point gave way in our cover, till standing between the drops was no longer possible. The water coursed down the underside of the boards, and dripped in our necks and formed puddles on our hat-brims. We shifted our guns and traps and viands, till there was no longer any choice of position, when the loaves and the fishes, the salt and the sugar, the pork and the butter, shared the same watery fate. The fire was gasping its last. Little rivulets coursed about it, and bore away the quenched but steaming coals on their bosoms. The spring run in the rear of our camp swelled so rapidly that part of the trout that had been hastily left lying on its banks again found themselves quite at home. For over two hours the floods came down. About four o'clock Orville, who had not yet come from the day's sport, appeared. To say Orville was wet is not much; he was better than that, — he had been washed and rinsed in at least half a dozen waters, and the trout that he bore dangling at the end of a string hardly knew that they had been out of their proper element.

But he brought welcome news. He had been two or three miles down the creek, and had seen a log building, — whether house or stable he did not know, but it had the appearance of having a good roof, which was inducement enough for us instantly to leave our present quarters. Our course lay along an old wood-road, and much of the time we were to our knees in water. The woods were literally flooded everywhere. Every little rill and springlet ran like a mill-tail, while the main stream rushed and roared, foaming, leaping, lashing, its volume increased fifty-fold. The water was not roily, but of a rich coffee-color, from the leachings of the woods. No more trout for the next three days! we thought, as we looked upon the rampant stream.

After we had labored and floundered along for about an hour, the road turned to the left, and in a little stumpy clearing near the creek a gable uprose on our view. It did not prove to be just such a place as poets love to contemplate. It required a greater effort of the imagination than any of us were then capable of to believe it had ever been a favorite resort of wood-nymphs or sylvan deities. It savored rather of the equine and the bovine. The bark-men had kept their teams there, horses on the one side and oxen on the other, and no Hercules had ever done duty in cleansing the stables. But there was a dry loft overhead with some straw, where we might get some sleep, in spite of the rain and the midges; a double layer of boards, standing at a very acute angle, would keep off the former, while the mingled refuse hay and muck beneath would nurse a smoke that would prove a thorough protection against the latter. And then, when Jim, the two-handed, mounting the trunk of a prostrate maple near by, had severed it thrice with easy and familiar stroke, and, rolling the logs in front of the shanty, had kindled a fire, which, getting the better of the dampness, soon cast a bright glow over all, shedding warmth and light even into the dingy stable, I consented to unsling my knapsack and accept the situation. The rain had ceased, and the sun shone out behind the woods. We had trout sufficient for present needs; and after my first meal in an ox-stall, I strolled out on the rude log bridge to watch the angry Neversink rush by. Its waters fell quite as rapidly as they rose, and before sundown it looked as if we might have fishing again on the morrow. We had better sleep that night than either night before, though there were two disturbing causes,— the smoke in the early part of it, and the cold in the latter. The "no-see-ems" left in disgust; and, though disgusted myself, I swallowed the smoke as best I could, and hugged my pallet of straw the closer. But the day dawned bright, and a plunge in the Neversink set me all right again. The creek, to our surprise and gratification, was only a little higher than before the rain, and some of the finest trout we had yet seen we caught that morning near camp.

We tarried yet another day and night at the old stable, but taking our meals outside squatted on the ground, which had now become quite dry. Part of the day I spent strolling about the woods, looking up old acquaintances among the birds, and, as always, half expectant of making some new ones. Curiously enough, the most abundant species were among those I had found rare in most other localities, namely, the small water-wagtail, the mourning ground warbler, and the yellow-bellied woodpecker. The latter seems to be the prevailing woodpecker through the woods of this region.

That night the midges, those motes that sting, held high carnival. We learned afterward, in the settlement below and from the barkpeelers, that it was the worst night ever experienced in that valley. We had done no fishing during the day, but had anticipated some fine sport about sundown. Accordingly Aaron and I started off between six and seven o'clock, one going upstream and the other down. The scene was charming. The sun shot up great spokes of light from behind the woods, and beauty, like a presence, pervaded the atmosphere. But torment, multiplied as the sands of the seashore, lurked in every tangle and thicket. In a thoughtless moment I removed my shoes and socks, and waded in the water to secure a fine trout that had accidentally slipped from my string and was helplessly floating with the current. This caused some delay and gave the gnats time to accumulate. Before I had got one foot half dressed I was enveloped in a black mist that settled upon my hands and neck and face, filling my ears with infinitesimal pipings and covering my flesh with infinitesimal bitings. I thought I should have to flee to the friendly fumes of the old stable, with "one stocking off and one stocking on;" but I got my shoe on at last, though not without many amusing interruptions and digressions.

In a few moments after this adventure I was in rapid retreat toward camp. Just as I reached the path leading from the shanty to the creek, my companion in the same ignoble flight reached it also, his hat broken and rumpled, and his sanguine countenance looking more sanguinary than I had ever before seen it, and his speech, also, in the highest degree inflammatory. His face and forehead were as blotched and swollen as if he had just run his head into a hornets' nest, and his manner as precipitate as if the whole swarm was still at his back.

No smoke or smudge which we ourselves could endure was sufficient in the earlier part of that evening to prevent serious annoyance from the same cause; but later a respite was granted us.

About ten o'clock, as we stood round our camp-fire, we were startled by a brief but striking display of the aurora borealis. My imagination had already been excited by talk of legends and of weird shapes and appearances, and when, on looking up toward the sky, I saw those pale, phantasmal waves of magnetic light chasing each other across the little opening above our heads, and at first sight seeming barely to clear the treetops, I was as vividly impressed as if I had caught a glimpse of a veritable spectre of the Neversink. The sky shook and trembled like a great white curtain.

After we had climbed to our loft and had lain down to sleep, another adventure befell us. This time a new and uninviting customer appeared upon the scene, the *genius loci* of the old stable, namely, the "fretful porcupine." We had seen the marks and work of these animals about the shanty, and had been careful each night to hang our traps, guns, etc., beyond their reach, but of the prickly night-walker himself we feared we should not get a view.

We had lain down some half hour, and I was just on the threshold of sleep, ready, as it were, to pass through the open door into the land of dreams, when I heard outside somewhere that curious sound,—a sound which I had heard every night I spent in these woods, not only on this but on former expeditions, and which I had settled in my mind as proceeding from the porcupine, since I knew the sounds our other common animals were likely to make,—a sound that might be either a gnawing on some hard, dry substance, or a grating of teeth, or a shrill grunting.

Orville heard it also, and, raising up on his elbow, asked, "What is that?"

"What the hunters call a 'porcupig,'" said I.

"Sure?"

"Entirely so."

"Why does he make that noise?"

"It is a way he has of cursing our fire," I replied. "I heard him last night also."

"Where do you suppose he is?" inquired my companion, showing a disposition to look him up.

"Not far off, perhaps fifteen or twenty yards from our fire, where the shadows begin to deepen."

Orville slipped into his trousers, felt for my gun, and in a moment had disappeared down through the scuttle hole. I had no disposition to follow him, but was rather annoyed than otherwise at the disturbance. Getting the direction of the sound, he went picking his way over the rough, uneven ground, and, when he got where the light failed him, poking every doubtful object with the end of his gun. Presently he poked a light grayish object, like a large round stone, which surprised him by moving off. On this hint he fired, making an incurable wound in the "porcupig," which, nevertheless, tried harder than ever to escape. I lay listening, when, close on the heels of the report of the gun, came excited shouts for a revolver. Snatching up my Smith and Wesson, I hastened, shoeless and hatless, to the scene of action, wondering what was up. I found my companion struggling to detain, with the end of the gun, an uncertain object that was trying to crawl off into the darkness. "Look out!" said Orville, as he saw my bare feet, "the quills are lying thick around here."

And so they were; he had blown or beaten them nearly all off the poor creature's back, and was in a fair way completely to disable my gun, the ramrod of which was already broken and splintered clubbing his victim. But a couple of shots from the revolver, sighted by a lighted match, at the head of the animal, quickly settled him.

He proved to be an unusually large Canada porcupine,—an old patriarch, gray and venerable, with spines three inches long, and weighing, I should say, twenty pounds. The build of this animal is much like that of the woodchuck, that is, heavy and pouchy. The nose is blunter than that of the woodchuck, the limbs stronger, and the tail broader and heavier. Indeed, the latter appendage is quite club-like, and the animal can, no doubt, deal a smart blow with it. An old hunter with whom I talked thought it aided them in climbing. They are inveterate gnawers, and spend much of their time in trees gnawing the bark. In winter one will take up its abode in a hemlock, and continue there till the tree is quite denuded.

The carcass emitted a peculiar, offensive odor, and, though very fat, was not in the least inviting as game. If it is part of the economy of nature for one animal to prey upon some other beneath it, then the poor devil has indeed a mouthful that makes a meal off the porcupine. Panthers and lynxes have essayed it, but have invariably left off at the first course, and have afterwards been found dead, or nearly so, with their heads puffed up like a pincushion, and the quills protruding on all sides. A dog that understands the business will manœuvre round the porcupine till he gets an opportunity to throw it over on its back, when he fastens on its quilless underbody. Aaron was puzzled to know how long-parted friends could embrace, when it was suggested that the quills could be depressed or elevated at pleasure.

The next morning boded rain; but we had become thoroughly sated with the delights of our present quarters, outside and in, and packed up our traps to leave. Before we had reached the clearing, three miles below, the rain set in, keeping up a lazy, monotonous drizzle till the afternoon.

The clearing was quite a recent one, made mostly by barkpeelers, who followed their calling in the mountains round about in summer, and worked in their shops making shingle in winter. The Biscuit Brook came in here from the west,—a fine, rapid trout stream six or eight miles in length, with plenty of deer in the mountains about its head. On its banks we found the house of an old woodman, to whom we had been directed for information about the section we proposed to traverse.

"Is the way very difficult," we inquired, "across from the Neversink into the head of the Beaver-kill?"

"Not to me; I could go it the darkest night ever was. And I can direct you so you can find the way without any trouble. You go down the Neversink about a mile, when you come to Highfall Brook, the first stream that comes down on the right. Follow up it to Jim Reed's shanty, about three miles. Then cross the stream, and on the left bank, pretty well up on the side of the mountain, you will find a wood-road, which was made by a fellow below here who stole some ash logs off the top of the ridge last winter and drew them out on the snow. When the road first begins to tilt over the mountain, strike down to your left, and you can reach the Beaverkill before sundown."

As it was then after two o'clock, and as the distance was six or eight of these terrible hunters' miles, we concluded to take a whole day to it, and wait till next morning. The Beaverkill flowed west, the Neversink south, and I had a mortal dread of getting entangled amid the mountains and valleys that lie in either angle.

Besides, I was glad of another and final opportunity to pay my respects to the finny tribes of the Neversink. At this point it was one of the finest trout streams I had ever beheld. It was so sparkling, its bed so free from sediment or impurities of any kind, that it had a new look, as if it had just come from the hand of its Creator. I tramped along its margin upward of a mile that afternoon, part of the time wading to my knees, and casting my hook, baited only with a trout's fin, to the opposite bank. Trout are real cannibals, and make no bones, and break none either, in lunching on each other. A friend of mine had several in his spring, when one day a large female trout gulped down one of her male friends, nearly one third her own size, and went around for two days with the tail of her liege lord protruding from her mouth! A fish's eye will do for bait, though the anal fin is better. One of the natives here told me that when he wished to catch large trout (and I judged he never fished for any other,—I never do), he used for bait the bullhead, or dart, a little fish an inch and a half or two inches long, that rests on the pebbles near shore and darts quickly, when disturbed, from point to point. "Put that on your hook," said he, "and if there is a big fish in the creek, he is bound to have it." But the darts were not easily found; the big fish, I concluded, had cleaned them all out; and, then, it was easy enough to supply our wants with a fin.

Declining the hospitable offers of the settlers, we spread our blankets that night in a dilapidated shingle-shop on the banks of the Biscuit Brook, first flooring the damp ground with the new shingle that lay piled in one corner. The place had a great-throated chimney with a tremendous expanse of fireplace within, that cried "More!" at every morsel of wood we gave it.

But I must hasten over this part of the ground, nor let the delicious flavor of the milk we had that morning for breakfast, and that was so delectable after four days of fish, linger on my tongue; nor yet tarry to set down the talk of that honest, weatherworn passer-by who paused before our door, and every moment on the point of resuming his way, yet stood for an hour and recited his adventures hunting deer and bears on these mountains. Having replenished our stock of bread and salt pork at the house of one of the settlers, midday found us at Reed's shanty, — one of those temporary structures erected by the bark jobber to lodge and board his "hands" near their work. Jim not being at home, we could gain no information from the "women folks" about the way, nor from the men who had just come in to dinner; so we pushed on, as near as we could, according to the instructions we had previously received. Crossing the creek, we forced our way up the side of the mountain, through a perfect *cheval-de-frise* of fallen and peeled hemlocks, and, entering the dense woods above, began to look anxiously about for the wood-road. My companions at first could see no trace of it; but knowing that a casual wood-road cut in winter, when there was likely to be two or three feet of snow on the ground, would present only the slightest indications to the eye in summer, I looked a little closer, and could make out a mark or two here and there. The larger trees had been avoided, and the axe used only on the small saplings and underbrush, which had been lopped off a couple of feet from the ground. By being constantly on the alert, we followed it till near the top of the mountain; but, when looking to see it "tilt" over the other side, it disappeared altogether. Some stumps of the black cherry were found, and a solitary pair of snow-shoes was hanging high and dry on a branch, but no further trace of human hands could we see. While we were resting here a couple of hermit thrushes, one of them with some sad defect in his vocal powers which barred him from uttering more than a few notes of his song, gave voice to the solitude of the place. This was the second instance in which I have observed a song-bird with apparently some organic defect in its instrument. The other case was that of a bobolink, which, hover in mid-air and inflate its throat as it might, could only force out a few incoherent notes. But the bird in each case presented this striking contrast to human examples of the kind, that it was apparently just as proud of itself, and just as well satisfied with its performance, as were its more successful rivals.

After deliberating some time over a pocket compass which I carried, we decided upon our course, and held on to the west. The descent was very gradual. Traces of bear and deer were noted at different points, but not a live animal was seen.

About four o'clock we reached the bank of a stream flowing west. Hail to the Beaverkill! and we pushed on along its banks. The trout were plenty, and rose quickly to the hook; but we held on our way, designing to go into camp about six o'clock. Many inviting places, first on one bank, then on the other, made us linger, till finally we reached a smooth, dry place overshadowed by balsam and hemlock, where the creek bent around a little flat, which was so entirely to our fancy that we unslung our knapsacks at once. While my companions were cutting wood and making other preparations for the night, it fell to my lot, as the most successful angler, to provide the trout for supper and breakfast. How shall I describe that wild, beautiful stream, with features so like those of all other mountain streams? And yet, as I saw it in the deep twilight of those woods on that June afternoon, with its steady, even flow, and its tranquil, many-voiced murmur, it made an impression upon my mind distinct and peculiar, fraught in an eminent degree with the charm of seclusion and remoteness. The solitude was perfect, and I felt that strangeness and insignificance which the civilized man must always feel when opposing himself to such a vast scene of silence and wildness. The trout were quite black, like all wood trout, and took the bait eagerly. I followed the stream till the deepening shadows warned me to turn back. As I neared camp, the fire shone far through the trees, dispelling the gathering gloom, but blinding my eyes to all obstacles at my feet. I was seriously disturbed on arriving to find that one of my companions had cut an ugly gash in his shin with the axe while felling a tree. As we did not carry a fifth wheel, it was not just the time or place to have any of our members crippled, and I had bodings of evil. But, thanks to the healing virtues of the balsam which must have adhered to the blade of the axe, and double thanks to the court-plaster with which Orville had supplied himself before leaving home, the wounded leg, by being favored that night and the next day, gave us little trouble.

That night we had our first fair and square camping out, — that is, sleeping on the ground with no shelter over us but the trees, — and it was in many respects the pleasantest night we spent in the woods. The weather was perfect and the place was perfect, and for the first time we were exempt from the midges and smoke; and then we appreciated the clean new page we had to work on. Nothing is so acceptable to the camper-out as a pure article in the way of woods and waters. Any admixture of human relics mars the spirit of the scene. Yet I am willing to confess that, before we were through those woods, the marks of an axe in a tree were a welcome sight. On resuming our march next day we followed the right bank of the Beaverkill, in order to strike a stream which flowed in from the north, and which was the outlet of Balsam Lake, the objective point of that day's march. The distance to the lake from our camp could not have been over six or seven miles; yet, traveling as we did, without path or guide, climbing up banks, plunging into ravines, making detours around swampy places, and forcing our way through woods choked up with much fallen and decayed timber, it seemed at least twice that distance, and the mid-afternoon sun was shining when we emerged into what is called the "Quaker Clearing," ground that I had been over nine years before, and that lies about two miles south of the lake. From this point we had a well-worn path that led us up a sharp rise of ground, then through level woods till we saw the bright gleam of the water through the trees.

I am always struck, on approaching these little mountain lakes, with the extensive preparation that is made for them in the conformation of the ground. I am thinking of a depression, or natural basin, in the side of the mountain or on its top, the brink of which I shall reach after a little steep climbing; but instead of that, after I have accomplished the ascent, I find a broad sweep of level or gently undulating woodland that brings me after a half hour or so to the lake, which lies in this vast lap like a drop of water in the palm of a man's hand.

Balsam Lake was oval-shaped, scarcely more than half a mile long and a quarter of a mile wide, but presented a charming picture, with a group of dark gray hemlocks filling the valley about its head, and the mountains rising above and beyond. We found a bough house in good repair, also a dug-out and paddle and several floats of logs. In the dug-out I was soon creeping along the shady side of the lake, where the trout were incessantly jumping for a species of black fly, that, sheltered from the slight breeze, were dancing in swarms just above the surface of the water. The gnats were there in swarms also, and did their best toward balancing the accounts by preying upon me while I preyed upon the trout which preyed upon the flies. But by dint of keeping my hands, face, and neck constantly wet, I am convinced that the balance of blood was on my side. The trout jumped most within a foot or two of shore, where the water was only a few inches deep. The shallowness of the water, perhaps, accounted for the inability of the fish to do more than lift their heads above the surface. They came up mouths wide open, and dropped back again in the most impotent manner. Where there is any depth of water, a trout will jump several feet into the air; and where there is a solid, unbroken sheet or column, they will scale falls and dams fifteen feet high.

We had the very cream and flower of our trout-fishing at this lake. For the first time we could use the fly to advantage; and then the contrast between laborious tramping along shore, on the one hand, and sitting in one end of a dug-out and casting your line right and left with no fear of entanglement in brush or branch, while you were gently propelled along, on the other, was of the most pleasing character.

There were two varieties of trout in the lake,—what it seems proper to call silver trout and golden trout; the former were the slimmer, and seemed to keep apart from the latter. Starting from the outlet and working round on the eastern side toward the head, we invariably caught these first. They glanced in the sun like bars of silver. Their sides and bellies were indeed as white as new silver. As we neared the head, and especially as we came near a space occupied by some kind of watergrass that grew in the deeper part of the lake, the other variety would begin to take the hook, their bellies a bright gold color, which became a deep orange on their fins; and as we returned to the place of departure with the bottom of the boat strewn with these bright forms intermingled, it was a sight not soon to be forgotten. It pleased my eye so, that I would fain linger over them, arranging them in rows and studying the various hues and tints. They were of nearly a uniform size, rarely one over ten or under eight inches in length, and it seemed as if the hues of all the precious metals and stones were reflected from their sides. The flesh was deep salmon-color; that of brook trout is generally much lighter. Some hunters and fishers from the valley of the Mill Brook, whom we met here, told us the trout were much larger in the lake, though far less numerous than they used to be. Brook trout do not grow large till they become scarce. It is only in streams that have been long and much fished that I have caught them as much as sixteen inches in length.

The "porcupigs" were numerous about the lake, and not at all shy. One night the heat became so intolerable in our oven-shaped bough house that I was obliged to withdraw from under its cover and lie down a little to one side. Just at daybreak, as I lay rolled in my blanket, something awoke me. Lifting up my head, there was a porcupine with his forepaws on my hips. He was apparently as much surprised as I was; and to my inquiry as to what he at that moment might be looking for, he did not pause to reply, but hitting me a slap with his tail which left three or four quills in my blanket, he scampered off down the hill into the brush.

Being an observer of the birds, of course every curious incident connected with them fell under my notice. Hence, as we stood about our camp-fire one afternoon looking out over the lake, I was the only one to see a little commotion in the water, half hidden by the near branches, as of some tiny swimmer struggling to reach the shore. Rushing to its rescue in the canoe, I found a yellow-rumped warbler, quite exhausted, clinging to a twig that hung down into the water. I brought the drenched and helpless thing to camp, and, putting it into a basket, hung it up to dry. An hour or two afterward I heard it fluttering in its prison, and cautiously lifted the lid to get a better glimpse of the lucky captive, when it darted out and was gone in a twinkling. How came it in the water? That was my wonder, and I can only guess that it was a young bird that had never before flown over a pond of water, and, seeing the clouds and blue sky so perfect down there, thought it was a vast opening or gateway into another summer land, perhaps a short cut to the tropics, and so got itself into trouble. How my eye was delighted also with the redbird that alighted for a moment on a dry branch above the lake, just where a ray of light from the setting sun fell full upon it! A mere crimson point, and yet how it offset that dark, sombre background!

I have thus run over some of the features of an ordinary trouting excursion to the woods. People inexperienced in such matters, sitting in their rooms and thinking of these things, of all the poets have sung and romancers written, are apt to get sadly taken in when they attempt to realize their dreams. They expect to enter a sylvan paradise of trout, cool retreats, laughing brooks, picturesque views, and balsamic couches, instead of which they find hunger, rain, smoke, toil, gnats, mosquitoes, dirt, broken rest, vulgar guides, and salt pork; and they are very apt not to see where the fun comes in. But he who goes in a right spirit will not be disappointed, and will find the taste of this kind of life better, though bitterer, than the writers have described.

Birch Browsings

The region of which I am about to speak lies in the southern part of the state of New York, and comprises parts of three counties,—Ulster, Sullivan and Delaware. It is drained by tributaries of both the Hudson and Delaware, and, next to the Adirondack section, contains more wild land than any other tract in the State. The mountains which traverse it, and impart to it its severe northern climate, belong properly to the Catskill range. On some maps of the State they are called the Pine Mountains, though with obvious local impropriety, as pine, so far as I have observed, is nowhere found upon them. "Birch Mountains" would be a more characteristic name, as on their summits birch is the prevailing tree. They are the natural home of the black and yellow birch, which grow here to unusual size. On their sides beech and maple abound; while, mantling their lower slopes and darkening the valleys, hemlock formerly enticed the lumberman and tanner. Except in remote or inaccessible localities, the latter tree is now almost never found. In Shandaken and along the Esopus it is about the only product the country yielded, or is likely to yield. Tanneries by the score have arisen and flourished upon the bark, and some of them still remain. Passing through that region the present season, I saw that the few patches of hemlock that still lingered high up on the sides of the mountains were being felled and peeled, the fresh white boles or the trees, just stripped of their bark, being visible a long distance.

Among these mountains there are no sharp peaks, or abrupt declivities, as in a volcanic region, but long, uniform ranges, heavily timbered to their summits, and delighting the eye with vast, undulating horizon lines. Looking south from the heights about the head of the Delaware, one sees, twenty miles away, a continual succession of blue ranges, one behind the other. If a few large trees are missing on the sky line, one can see the break a long distance off.

Approaching this region from the Hudson River side, you cross a rough, rolling stretch of country, skirting the base of the Catskills, which from a point near Saugerties sweep inland; after a drive of a few hours you are within the shadow of a high, bold mountain, which forms a sort of butt-end to this part of the range, and which is simple called High Point. To the east and southeast it slopes down rapidly to the plain, and looks defiance toward the Hudson, twenty miles distant; in the rear of it, and radiating from it west and northwest, are numerous smaller ranges, backing up, as it were, this haughty chief.

From this point through to Pennsylvania, a distance of nearly one hundred miles, stretches the tract of which I speak. It is a belt of country from twenty to thirty miles wide, bleak and wild, and but sparsely settled. The traveler on the New York and Erie Railroad gets a glimpse of it.

Many cold, rapid trout streams, which flow to all points of the compass, have their source in the small lakes and copious mountain springs of this region. The names of some of them are Mill Brook, Dry Brook, Willewemack, Beaver Kill, Elk Bush Kill, Panther Kill, Neversink, Big Ingin, and Callikoon. Beaver Kill is the main outlet on the west. It joins the Deleware in the wilds of Hancock. The Neversink lays open the region to the south, and also joins the Delaware. To the east, various Kills unite with the Big Ingin to form the Esopus, which flows into the Hudson. Dry Brook and Mill Brook, both famous trout streams, from twelve to fifteen miles long, find their way into the Delaware.

The east or Pepacton branch of the Delaware itself takes its rise near here in a deep pass between the mountains. I have many times drunk at a copious spring by the roadside, where the infant river first sees the light. A few yards beyond, the water flows the other way, directing its course through the Bear Kill and Schoharie Kill into the Mohawk.

Such game and wild animals as still linger in the State are found in this region. Bears occasionally make havoc among the sheep. The clearings at the head of a valley are oftenest the scene of their depredations.

Wild pigeons, in immense numbers used to breed regularly in the valley of the Big Ingin and about the head of the Neversink. The treetops for miles were full of their nests, while the going and coming of the old birds kept up a constant din. But the gunners soon got wind of it, and from far and near were wont to pour in during the spring, and to slaughter both old and young. This practice soon had the effect of driving the pigeons all away, and now only a few pairs breed in these woods.

Deer are still met with, though they are becoming scarcer every year. Last winter near seventy head were killed on the Beaver Kill alone. I heard of one wretch, who, finding the deer snowbound, walked up to them on his snowshoes, and one morning before breakfast slaughtered six, leaving their carcasses where they fell. There are traditions of persons having been smitten blind or senseless when about to commit some heinous offense, but the fact that this villain escaped without some such visitation throws discredit on all such stories.

The great attraction, however, of this region, is the brook trout, with which the streams and lakes abound. The water is of excessive coldness, the thermometer indicating 44° and 45°in the springs, and 47° or 48° in the smaller streams. The trout are generally small, but in the more remote branches their number is very great. In such localities the fish are quite black, but in the lakes they are of a lustre and brilliancy impossible to describe.

These waters have been much visited of late years by fishing parties, and the name of the Beaver Kill is now a potent name among New York sportsmen.

One lake, in the wilds of Callikoon, abounds in a peculiar species of white sucker, which is of excellent quality. It is taken only in spring, during the spawning season, at the time "when the leaves are as big as a chipmunk's ears." The fish run up the small streams and inlets, beginning at nightfall, and continuing till the channel is literally packed with them, and every inch of space is occupied. The fishermen pounce upon them at such times, and scoop them up by the bushel, usually wading right into the living mass and landing the fish with their hands. A small party will often secure in this manner a wagon-load of fish. Certain conditions of the weather, as a warm south or southwest wind, are considered most favorable for the fish to run.

Though familiar all my life with the outskirts of this region, I have only twice dipped into its wilder portions. Once in 1860 a friend and myself traced the Beaver Kill to its source, and encamped by Balsam Lake. A cold and protracted rainstorm coming on, we were obliged to leave the woods before we were ready. Neither of us will soon forget that tramp by an unknown route over the mountains, encumbered as we were with a hundred and one superfluities which we had foolishly brought along to solace ourselves with in the woods; nor that halt on the summit, where we cooked and ate our fish in the drizzling rain; nor, again, that rude log house, with its sweet hospitality, which we reached just at nightfall on Mill Brook.

In 1868 a party of three of us set out for a brief trouting excursion to a body of water called Thomas's Lake, situated in the same chain of mountains. On this excursion, more particularly than on any other I have ever undertaken, I was taught how poor an Indian I should make, and what a ridiculous figure a party of men may cut in the woods when the way is uncertain and the mountains high.

We left our team at a farmhouse near the head of the Mill Brook, one June afternoon, and with knapsacks on our shoulders struck into the woods at the base of the mountain, hoping to cross the range that intervened between us and the lake by sunset. We engaged a good-natured but rather indolent young man, who happened to be stopping at the house, and who had carried a knapsack in the Union armies, to pilot us a couple of miles into the woods so as to guard against any mistakes at the outset. It seemed the easiest thing in the world to find the lake. The lay of the land was so simple, according to accounts, that I felt sure I could go it in the dark. "Go up this little brook to its source on the side of the mountain," they said. "The valley that contains the lake heads directly on the other side." What could be easier! But on a little further inquiry, they said we should "bear well to the left" when we reached the top of the mountain. This opened the doors again; "bearing well to the left" was an uncertain performance in strange woods. We might bear so well to the left that it would bring us ill. But why bear to the left at all, if the lake was directly opposite? Well, not quite opposite; a little to the left. There were two or three other valleys that headed in near there. We could easily find the right one. But to make assurance doubly sure, we engaged a guide, as stated, to give us a good start, and go with us beyond the bearing-to-the-left point. He had been to the lake the winter before and knew the way. Our course, the first half hour, was along an obscure wood-road which had been used for drawing ash logs off mountain in winter. There was some hemlock, but more maple and birch. The woods were dense and free from underbrush, the ascent gradual. Most of the way we kept the voice of the creek in our ear on the right. I approached it once, and found it swarming with trout. The water was as cold as one ever need wish. After a while the ascent grew steeper, the creek became a mere rill that issued from beneath loose, moss-covered rocks and stones, and with much labor and puffing we drew ourselves up the rugged declivity. Every mountain has its steepest point, which is usually near the summit, in keeping, I suppose, with the providence that makes the darkest hour just before day. It is steep, steeper, steepest, till you emerge on the smooth level or gently rounded space at the top, which the old ice-gods polished off so long ago.

We found this mountain had a hollow in its back where the ground was soft and swampy. Some gigantic ferns, which we passed through, came nearly to our shoulders. We passed also several patches of swamp honeysuckles, red with blossoms.

Our guide at length paused on a big rock where the land begin to dip down the other way, and concluded that he had gone far enough, and that we would now have no difficulty in finding the lake. "It must lie right down there," he said pointing with his hand. But it was plain that he was not quite sure in his own mind. He had several times wavered in his course, and had shown considerable embarrassment when bearing to the left across the summit. Still we thought little of it. We were full of confidence, and bidding him adieu, plunged down the mountain-side, following a spring run that we had no doubt left to the lake.

In these woods, which had a southeastern exposure, I first began to notice the wood thrush. In coming up the other side, I had not seen a feather of any kind, or heard a note. Now the golden trillide-de of the wood thrush sounded through the silent woods. While looking for a fish-pole about halfway down the mountain, I saw a thrush's nest in a little sapling about ten feet from the ground.

After continuing our descent till our only guide, the spring run, became quite a trout brook, and its tiny murmur a loud brawl, we began to peer anxiously through the trees for a glimpse of the lake, or for some conformation of the land that would indicate its proximity. An object which we vaguely discerned in looking under the near trees and over the more distant ones proved, on further inspection, to be a patch of plowed ground. Presently we made out a burnt fallow near it. This was a wet blanket to our enthusiasm. No lake, no sport, no trout for supper that night. The rather indolent young man had either played us a trick, or, as seemed more likely, had missed the way. We were particularly anxious to be at the lake between sundown and dark, as at that time the trout jump most freely.

Pushing on, we soon emerged into a stumpy field, at the head of a steep valley, which swept around toward the west. About two hundred rods below us was a rude log house, with smoke issuing from the chimney. A boy came out and moved toward the spring with a pail in his hand. We shouted to him, when he turned and ran back into the house without pausing to reply. In a moment the whole family hastily rushed into the yard, and turned their faces toward us. If we had come down their chimney, they could not have seemed more astonished. Not making out what they said, I went down to the house, and learned to my chagrin that we were still on the Mill Brook side, having crossed only a spur of the mountain. We had not borne sufficiently to the left, so that the main range, which, at the point of crossing, suddenly breaks off to the southeast, still intervened between us and the lake. We were about five miles, as the water runs, from the point of starting, and over two from the lake. We must go directly back to the top of the range where the guide had left us, and then, by keeping well to the left, we would soon come to a line of marked trees, which would lead us to the lake. So, turning upon our trail, we doggedly began the work of undoing what we had just done,—in all cases a disagreeable task, in this case a very laborious one also. It was after sunset when we turned back, and before we had got halfway up the mountain, it began to be quite dark. We were often obliged to rest our packs against the trees and take breath, which made our progress slow. Finally a halt was called, beside an immense flat rock which had paused on its slide down the mountain, and we prepared to encamp for the night. A fire was built the rock cleared off, a small ration of bread served out, our accoutrements hung up out of the way of the hedgehogs that were supposed to infest the locality, and then we disposed ourselves for sleep. If the owls or porcupines (and I think I heard one of the latter in the middle of the night) reconnoitered our camp, they saw a buffalo robe spread upon a rock, with three old felt hats arranged on one side, and three pairs of sorry-looking cowhide boots protruding from the other.

When we lay down, there was apparently not a mosquito in the woods; but the "no-see-ems," as Thoreau's Indian aptly named the midges, soon found us out, and after the fire had gone down, annoyed us very much. My hands and wrists suddenly began to smart and itch in a most uncomfortable manner. My first thought was that they had been poisoned in some way. Then the smarting extended to my neck and face, even to my scalp, when I began to suspect what was the matter. So, wrapping myself up more thoroughly, and stowing my hands away as best I could, I tried to sleep, being some time behind my companions, who appeared not to mind the "no-see-ems." I was further annoyed by some little irregularity on my side of the couch. The chambermaid had not beaten it up well. One huge lump refused to be mollified, and each attempt to adapt it up some natural hollow in my own body brought only a moment's relief. But at last I got the better of this also and slept. Late in the night I woke up, just in time to hear a golden-crowned thrush sing in a tree near by. It sang as loud and cheerily as at midday, and I thought myself, after all, quite in luck. Birds occasionally sing at night, just as the cock crows. I have heard the hairbird, and the note of the kingbird; and the ruffed grouse frequently drums at night.

At the first faint signs of day a wood thrush sang, a few rods below us. Then after a little delay, as the gray light began to grow around, thrushes broke out in full song in all parts of the woods. I thought I had never before heard them sing so sweetly. Such a leisurely, golden chant! —it consoled us for all we had undergone. It was the first thing in order,—the worms were safe till after this morning chorus. I judged that the birds roosted but a few feet from the ground. In fact, a bird in all cases roosts where it builds, and the wood thrush occupies, as it were, the first story of the woods.

There is something singular about the distribution of the wood thrushes. At an earlier stage of my observations I should have been much surprised at finding them in these woods. Indeed, I had stated in print on two occasions that the wood thrush was not found in the higher lands of the Catskills, but that the hermit thrush and the veery, or Wilson's thrush, were common. It turns out that the statement is only half true. The wood thrush is found also, but is much more rare and secluded in its habits than either of the others, being seen only during the breeding season on remote mountains, and then only on their eastern and southern slopes. I have never yet in this region found the bird spending the season in the near and familiar woods, which is directly contrary to observations I have made in other parts of the state. So different are the habits of birds in different localities.

As soon as it was fairly light we were up and ready to resume our march. A small bit of bread and butter and a swallow or two of whiskey was all we had for breakfast that morning. Our supply of each was very limited, and we were anxious to save a little of both, to relieve the diet of trout to which we looked forward.

At an early hour we reached the rock where we had parted with the guide, and looked around us into the dense, trackless woods with many misgivings. To strike out now on our own hook, where the way was so blind and after the experience we had just had, was a step not to be carelessly taken. The tops of these mountains are so broad, and a short distance in the woods seems so far, that one is by no means master of the situation after reaching the summit. And then there are so many spurs and offshoots and changes of direction, added to the impossibility of making any generalization by the aid of the eye, that before one is aware of it he is very wide of his mark.

I remembered now that a young farmer of my acquaintance had told me how he had made a long day's march through the heart of this region, without path or guide of any kind, and had hit his mark squarely. He had been barkpeeling in Callikoon,—a famous country for barkpeeling,—and, having got enough of it, he desired to reach his home on Dry Brook without making the usual circuitous journey between the two places. To do this necessitated a march of ten or twelve miles across several ranges of mountains and through an unbroken forest, —a hazardous undertaking in which no one would join him. Even the old hunters who were familiar with the ground dissuaded him and predicted the failure of his enterprise. But having made up his mind, he possessed himself thoroughly of the topography of the country from the aforesaid hunters, shouldered his axe, and set out, holding a strait course through the woods, and turning aside for neither swamps, streams, nor mountains. When he paused to rest he would mark some object ahead of him with his eye, in order that on getting up again, he might not deviate from his course. His directors had told him of a hunter's cabin about midway on his route, which if he struck he might be sure he was right. About noon this cabin was reached, and at sunset he emerged at the head of Dry Brook.

After looking in vain for the line of marked trees, we moved off to the left in a doubtful, hesitating manner, keeping on the highest ground and blazing the trees as we went. We were afraid to go downhill, lest we should descend to soon; our vantage-ground was high ground. A thick fog coming on, we were more bewildered than ever. Still we pressed forward, climbing up ledges and wading through ferns for about two hours, when we paused by a spring that issued from beneath an immense wall of rock that belted the highest part of the mountain. There was quite a broad plateau here, and the birch wood was very dense, and the trees of unusual size.

After resting and exchanging opinions, we all concluded that is was best not to continue our search encumbered as we were; but we were not willing to abandon it altogether, and I proposed to my companions to leave them beside the spring with our traps, while I made one thorough and final effort to find the lake. If I succeeded and desired them to come forward, I was to fire my gun three times; if I failed and wished to return, I would fire twice, they of course responding.

So, filling my canteen from the spring, I set out again, taking the spring run for my guide. Before I had followed it two hundred yards, it sank into the ground at my feet. I had half a mind to be superstitious and to believe that we were under a spell, since our guides played us such tricks. However, I determined to put the matter to a further test, and struck out boldly to the left. This seemed to be the keyword,—to the left, to the left. The fog had now lifted, so that I could form a better idea of the lay of the land. Twice I looked down the steep sides of the mountain, sorely attempted to risk a plunge. Still I hesitated and kept along on the brink. As I stood on a rock deliberating, I heard a crackling of the brush, like the tread of some large game, on the plateau below me. Suspecting the truth of the case, I moved stealthily down, and found a herd of young cattle leisurely browsing. We had several times crossed their trail, and had seen that morning a level, grassy place on the top of the mountain, where they had passed the night. Instead of being frightened, as I had expected, they seemed greatly delighted, and gathered around me as if to inquire the tidings from the outer world,—perhaps the quotations of the cattle market. They came up to me, and eagerly licked my hand, clothes, and gun. Salt was what they were after, and they were ready to swallow anything that contained the smallest percentage of it. They were mostly yearlings and as sleek as moles. They had a very gamy look. We were afterwards told that, in the spring, the farmers round about turn into these woods their young cattle, which do not come out again till fall. They are then in good condition,—not fat, like grass-fed cattle, but trim and supple, like deer. Once a month the owner hunts them up and salts them. They have their beats, and seldom wander beyond well-defined limits. It was interesting to see them feed. They browsed on the low limbs and bushes, and on the various plants, munching at everything without any apparent discrimination.

They attempted to follow me, but I escaped them by clambering down some steep rocks. I now found myself gradually edging down the side of the mountain, keeping around it in a spiral manner, and scanning the woods and the shape of the ground for some encouraging hint or sign. Finally the woods became more open, and the descent less rapid. The trees were remarkably straight and uniform in size. Black birches, the first I had ever seen, were very numerous. I felt encouraged. Listening attentively, I caught, from a breeze just lifting the drooping leaves, a sound that I willingly believed was made by a bullfrog. On this hint, I tore down through the woods at my highest speed. Then I paused and listened again. This time there was no mistaking it; it was the sound of frogs. Much elated, I rushed on. By and by I could hear them as I ran.

Pthrung, pthrung, croaked the old ones; pug, pug, shrilly joined in the smaller fry.

Then I caught, through the lower trees, a gleam of blue, which I first thought was distant sky. A second look and I knew it to be water, and in a moment more I stepped from the woods and stood upon the shore of the lake. I exulted silently. There it was at last, sparkling in the morning sun, and as beautiful as a dream. It was so good to come upon such open space and such bright hues, after wandering in the dim, dense woods! The eye is as delighted as an escaped bird, and darts gleefully from point to point.

The lake was a long oval, scarcely more than a mile in circumference, with evenly wooded shores, which rose gradually on all sides. After contemplating the serene for a moment, I stepped back into the woods, and, loading my gun as heavily as I dared, discharged it three times. The reports seemed to fill all the mountains with sound. The frogs quickly hushed, and I listened for the response. But no response came. Then I tried again and again, but without evoking an answer. One of my companions, however, who had climbed to the top of the high rocks in the rear of the spring, thought he heard faintly one report. It seemed an immense distance below him, and far around under the mountain. I knew I had come a long way, and hardly expected to be able to communicate with my companions in the manner agreed upon. I therefore started back, choosing my course without any reference to the circuitous route by which I had come, and loading heavily

and firing at intervals. I must have aroused many long-
dormant echoes from a Rip Van Winkle sleep. As my
powder got low, I fired and hallooed alternately, till I cam
near splitting both my throat and gun. Finally, after I had
begun to have a very ugly feeling of alarm and
disappointment, and to cast about vaguely for some course
to pursue in an emergency that seemed near at hand,—
namely the loss of my companions now I had found the
lake,—a favoring breeze brought me the last echo of a
response. I rejoined with spirit, and hastened with all
speed in the direction whence the sound had come, but,
after repeated trials, failed to elicit another answering
sound. This filled me with apprehension again. I feared
that my friends had been mislead by the reverberations,
and I pictured them to myself, hastening in the opposite
direction. Paying little attention to my course, but paying
dearly for my carelessness afterward, I rushed forward to
undeceive them. But they had not been deceived, and in a
few moments an answering shout revealed them near at
hand. I heard their tramp, the bushed parted, and we three
met again.

In answer to their eager inquiries, I assured them that
I had seen the lake, that it was at the foot of the mountain,
and that we could not miss it if we kept straight down
from where we then were.

My clothes were soaked in perspiration, but I
shouldered my knapsack with alacrity, and we began the
descent. I noticed that the woods were much thicker, and
had quite a different look from those I had passed through,

but thought nothing of it, as I expected to strike the lake near its head, whereas I had before come out at its foot. We had not gone far when we crossed a line of marked trees, which my companions were disposed to follow. It intersected our course nearly at right angles, and kept along and up the side of the mountain. My impression was that it lead up from the lake, and that by keeping our course we should reach the lake sooner than if we followed this line. About halfway down the mountain, we could see through the interstices the opposite slope. I encouraged my comrades by telling them that the lake was between us and that, and not more than half a mile distant. We soon reached the bottom, where we found a small stream and quite an extensive alder swamp, evidently the ancient bed of a lake. I explained to my half-vexed and half-incredulous companions that we were probably above the lake, and that this stream must lead to it. "Follow it," they said; "we will wait here till we hear from you."

So I went on, more than ever disposed to believe that we were under a spell, and that the lake had slipped from my grasp after all. Seeing no favorable sign as I went forward, I laid down my accoutrements, and climbed a decayed beech that leaned out over the swamp and promised a good view from the top. As I stretched myself up to look around from the highest attainable branch, there was suddenly a loud crack at the root. With a celerity that would at least have done credit to a bear, I regained the ground, having caught but a momentary glimpse of the country, but enough to convince me no lake was near. Leaving all incumbrances here but my gun, I still pressed on, loath to be thus baffled. After floundering through another alder swamp for nearly half a mile, I flattered myself that I was close to the lake. I caught sight of a low spur of the mountain sweeping around like a half-extended arm, and I fondly imagined that within its clasp was the object of my search. But I found only more alder swamp. After this region was cleared the creek began to descend the mountain very rapidly. Its banks became high and narrow, and it went whirling away with a sound that seemed to my ears like a burst of ironical laughter. I turned back with a feeling of mingled disgust, shame and vexation. In fact I was almost sick, and when I reached my companions, after an absence of nearly two hours, hungry, fatigued, and disheartened, I would have sold my interest in Thomas's Lake at a very low figure. For the first time, I heartily wished myself well out of the woods. Thomas might keep his lake, and the enchanters guard his possession! I doubted if he had ever found it the second time, or if any one else ever had.

My companions, who were quite fresh and who had not felt the strain of baffled purpose as I had, assumed a more encouraging tone. After I had rested awhile, and partaken sparingly of the bread and whisky, which in such an emergency is a great improvement on bread and water, I agreed to their proposition that we should make another attempt. As if to reassure us, a robin sounded his cheery call near by, and the winter wren, the first I had ever heard in these woods, set his music-box going, which fairly ran over with fin, gushing, lyrical sounds. There can be no doubt but this bird is one of our finest songsters. If it would only thrive and sing well when caged, like the canary, how far it would surpass that bird! It has all the vivacity and versatility of the canary, without any of its shrillness. Its song is indeed a little cascade of melody.

We again retraced our steps, rolling the stone, as it were, back up the mountain, determined to commit ourselves to the line of marked trees. These we finally reached, and, after exploring the country to the right, saw that bearing to the left was still the order. The trail led up over a gentle rise of ground, and in less than twenty minutes, we were in the woods I had passed through when I found the lake. The error I had made was then plain: we had come off the mountain a few paces too far to the right, and so had passed down on the wrong side of the ridge, into what we afterwards learned was the valley of Alder Creek.

We now made good time, and before many minutes I again saw the mimic sky glance through the trees. As we approached the lake, a solitary woodchuck, the first wild animal we had seen since entering the woods, sat crouched upon the root of a tree a few feet from the water, apparently completely nonplussed by the unexpected appearance of danger on the land side. All retreat was cut off, and he looked his fate in the face without flinching. I slaughtered him just as a savage would have done, and from the same motive, — I wanted his carcass to eat.

The mid-afternoon sun was now shining upon the lake, and a low, steady breeze drove the little waves rocking to the shore. A herd of cattle were browsing on the other side, and the bell of the leader sounded across the water. In these solitudes its clang was wild and musical.

To try the trout was the first thing in order. On a rude raft of log which we found moored at the shore, and which with two aboard shipped about a food of water, we floated out and wet our first fly in Thomas's Lake; but the trout refused to jump, and to be frank, not more than a dozen and a half were caught during our stay. Only a week previous, a party of three had taken in a few hours all the fish they could carry out of the woods, and had nearly surfeited their neighbors with trout. But from some cause, they now refused to rise, or to touch any kind of bait: so we fell to catching the sunfish, which were small but very abundant. Their nests were all along the shore. A space about the size of a breakfast-plate was cleared of sediment and decayed vegetable matter, revealing the pebbly bottom, fresh and bright, with one or two fish suspended over the centre of it, keeping watch and ward. If an intruder approached, they would dart at him spitefully. These fish have the air of bantam cocks, and, with their sharp, prickly fins and spines and scaly sides, must be ugly customers in a hand-to-hand encounter with other finny warriors. To a hungry man they look about as unpromising as hemlock slivers, so thorny and thin are they; yet there is sweet meat in them, as we found that day.

Much refreshed, I set out with the sun low in the west to explore the outlet of the lake and try for trout there, while my companions made further trials in the lake itself.

The outlet, as is usual in bodies of water of this kind, was very gentle and private. The stream, six or eight feet wide, flowed silently and evenly along for a distance of three or four rods, when it suddenly, as if conscious of its freedom, took a leap down some rocks. Thence as far as I followed it, its decent was very rapid through a continuous succession of brief falls like so many steps down the mountain. Its appearance promised more trout than I found, though I returned to camp with a very respectable string.

Toward sunset I went round to explore the inlet, and found that as usual the stream wound leisurely through marshy ground. The water being much colder than in the outlet, the trout were more plentiful. As I was picking my way over the miry ground and through the rank growths, a ruffed grouse hopped up on a fallen branch a few paces before me, and jerking his tail, threatened to take flight. But as I was at the moment gunless and remained stationary, he presently jumped down and walked away.

A seeker of birds, and ever on the alert for some new acquaintance, my attention was arrested, on first entering the swamp, by a bright, lively song, or warble, that issued from the branches overhead, and that was entirely new to me, though there was something in the tone that told me the bird was related to the wood-wagtail and to the water-wagtail or thrush. The strain was emphatic and quite loud, like the canary's, but very brief. The bird kept itself well secreted in the upper branches of the trees, and for a long time eluded my eye. I passed to and fro several times, and it seemed to break out afresh as I approached a certain little bend in the creek, and to cease after I had got beyond it; no doubt its nest was somewhere in the vicinity. After some delay the bird was sighted and brought down. It proved to be the small, or northern, water-thrush, (called also the New York water-thrush),—a new bird to me. In size it was noticeably smaller than the large, or Louisiana, water-thrush, as described by Audubon, but in other respects its general appearance was the same. It was a great treat to me, and again I felt myself in luck.

This bird was unknown to the older ornithologists, and is but poorly described by the new. It builds a mossy nest on the ground, or under the edge of a decayed log. A correspondent writes me that he has found it breeding on the mountains in Pennsylvania. The large-billed water-thrush is much the superior songster, but the present species has a very bright and cheerful strain. The specimen I saw, contrary to the habits of the family, kept in the treetops like a warbler, and seemed to be engaged in catching insects.

The birds were unusually plentiful and noisy about the head of this lake; robins, blue jays, and woodpeckers greeted me with their familiar notes. The blue jays found an owl or some wild animal a short distance above me, and, as is their custom on such occasions, proclaimed it at the top of their voices, and kept on till the darkness began to gather in the woods.

I also heard, as I had at two or three other points in the course of the day, the peculiar, resonant hammering of some species of woodpecker upon the hard, dry limbs. It was unlike any sound of the kind I had ever heard, and, repeated at intervals through the silent wood, was a very marked and characteristic feature. Its peculiarity was the ordered succession of the raps, which gave it the character of a premeditated performance. There were first three strokes following each other rapidly, then two much louder ones with longer intervals between them. I heard the drumming here, and the next day at sunset at Furlow Lake, the source of Dry Brook, and in no instance was the order varied. There was a melody in it, such as a woodpecker knows how to evoke from a smooth, dry branch. It suggested something quite as pleasing as the liveliest bird-song, and was if anything more woodsy and wild. As the yellow-bellied woodpecker was the most abundant species in these woods, I attributed it to him. It is the one sound that still links itself with those scenes in my mind.

At sunset the grouse began to drum in all parts of the woods about the lake. I could hear five at one time, thump, thump, thump, thump, thr-r-r-r-r-rr. It was a homely, welcome sound. As I returned to camp at twilight, along the shore of the lake, the frogs also were in full chorus. The older ones ripped out their responses to each other with terrific force and volume. I know of no other animal capable of giving forth so much sound, in proportion to its size, as a frog. Some of these seemed to bellow as loud as a two-year-old bull. They were of immense size, and very abundant. No frog-eater had ever been there. Near the shore we felled a tree which reached far out in the lake.

Upon the trunk and branches, the frogs soon collected in large numbers, and gamboled and splashed about the half submerged top, like a parcel of schoolboys, making nearly as much noise.

After dark, as I was frying the fish, a panful of the largest trout was accidentally capsized in the fire. With rueful countenances we contemplated the irreparable loss our commissariat had sustained by this mishap; but remembering there was virtue in ashes, we poked the half-consumed fish from the bed of coals and ate them, and they were good.

We lodged that night on a brush-heap and slept soundly. The green, yielding beech-twigs, covered with a buffalo robe, were equal to a hair mattress. The heat and smoke from a large fire kindled in the afternoon had banished every "no-see-em" from the locality, and in the morning the sun was above the mountain before we awoke.

I immediately started again for the inlet, and went far up the stream toward its source. A fair string of trout for breakfast was my reward. The cattle with the bell were at the head of the valley, where they had passed the night. Most of them were two-year-old steers. They came up to me and begged for salt, and scared the fish by their importunities.

We finished our bread that morning, and ate every fish we could catch, and about ten o'clock prepared to leave the lake. The weather had been admirable, and the lake as a gem, and I would gladly have spent a week in the neighborhood; but the question of supplies was a serious one, and would brook no delay.

When we reached, on our return, the point where we had crossed the line of marked trees the day before, the question arose whether we should still trust ourselves to this line, or follow our own trail back to the spring and the battlement of rocks on the top of the mountain, and thence to the rock where the guide had left us. We decided in favor of the former course. After a march of three quarters of an hour the blazed trees ceased, and we concluded we were near the point at which we had parted with our guide. So we built a fire, laid down our loads, and cast about on all sides for some clew as to our exact locality. Nearly an hour was consumed in this manner, and without any result. I came upon a brood of young grouse, which diverted me for a moment. The old one blustered about at a furious rate, trying to draw all attention to herself, while the young ones, which were unable to fly, hid themselves. She whined like a dog in great distress, and dragged herself along apparently with the greatest difficulty. As I pursued her, she ran very nimbly, and presently flew a few yards. Then, as I went on, she flew farther and farther each time, till at last she got up, and went humming through the woods as if she had no interest in them. I went back and caught one of the young, which had simply squatted close to the ground. I then put in my coatsleeve, when it ran and nestled in my armpit.

When we met at the sign of the smoke, opinions differed as to the most feasible course. There was no doubt but that we could get out of the woods; but we wished to get out speedily, and as near as possible to the point where we had entered. Half ashamed of our timidity and indecision, we finally tramped away back to where we had crossed the line of blazed trees, followed our old trail to the spring on the top of the range, and, after much searching and scouring to the right and left, found ourselves at the very place we had left two hours before. Another deliberation and a divided council. But something must be done. It was then mid-afternoon, and the prospect of spending another night on the mountains, without food or drink, was not pleasant. So we moved down the ridge. Here another line of marked trees was found, the course of which formed an obtuse angle with the one we had followed. It kept on the top of the ridge for perhaps a mile, when it disappeared, and we were as much adrift as ever. Then one of the party swore an oath, and said he was going out of those woods, hit or miss, and, wheeling to the right, instantly plunged over the brink of the mountain. The rest followed, but would fain have paused and ciphered away at their own uncertainties, to see if a certainty could not be arrived at as to where we would come out. But our bold leader was solving the problem in the right way. Down and down and still down we went, as if we were to bring up in the bowels of the earth. It was by far the steepest descent we had made, and we felt a grim satisfaction in knowing we could not retrace our steps this time, be the issue what it might. As we paused on the brink of a ledge of rocks, we chanced to see through the trees distant cleared land. A house or barn also was dimly descried. This was encouraging; but we could not make out whether it was on Beaver Kill or Mill Brook or Dry Brook, and did not long stop to consider where it was. We at last brought up at the bottom of a deep gorge, through which flowed a rapid creek that literally swarmed with trout. But we were in no mood to catch them, and pushed on along the channel of the stream, sometimes leaping from rock to rock, and sometimes splashing heedlessly through the water, and speculating the while as to where we should probably come out. On the Beaver Kill, my companions thought; but from the position of the sun, I said, on the Mill Brook, about six miles below our team; for I remembered having seen, in coming up this stream, a deep, wild valley that led up into the mountains, like this one. Soon the banks of the stream became lower, and we moved into the woods. Here we entered upon an obscure wood-road, which presently conducted us into the midst of a vast hemlock forest. The land had a gentle slope, and we wondered by the lumbermen and barkmen who prowl through these woods had left this fine tract untouched. Beyond this the forest was mostly birch and maple.

We were now close to settlement, and began to hear human sounds. One rod more, and we were out of the woods. It took us a moment to comprehend the scene. Things looked very strange at first; but quickly they began to change and to put on familiar features. Some magic scene-shifting seemed to take place before my eyes, till, instead of the unknown settlement which I had at first seemed to look upon, there stood the farmhouse at which we had stopped two days before, and at the same moment we heard the stamping of our team in the barn. We sat down and laughed heartily over our good luck. Our desperate venture had resulted better than we had dared to hope, and had shamed our wisest plans. At the house our arrival had been anticipated about this time, and dinner was being put upon the table.

It was then five o'clock, so that we had been in the woods just forty-eight hours; but if time is only phenomenal, as the philosophers say, and life only in feeling, as the poets aver, we were some months, if not years, older at that moment than we had been two days before. Yet younger, too,—though this be a paradox,—for the birches had infused into us some of their own suppleness and strength.

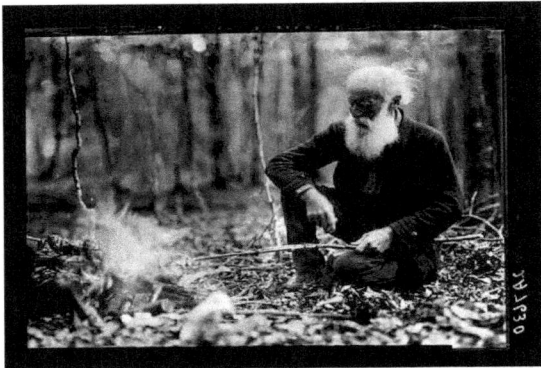

Notes By The Way

I. THE WEATHER-WISE MUSKRAT

I am more than half persuaded that the muskrat is a wise little animal, and that on the subject of the weather, especially, he possesses some secret that I should be glad to know. In the fall of 1878 I noticed that he built unusually high and massive nests. I noticed them in several different localities. In a shallow, sluggish pond by the roadside, which I used to pass daily in my walk, two nests were in process of construction throughout the month of November. The builders worked only at night, and I could see each day that the work had visibly advanced. When there was a slight skim of ice over the pond, this was broken up about the nests, with trails through it in different directions where the material had been brought. The houses were placed a little to one side of the main channel, and were constructed entirely of a species of coarse wild grass that grew all about. So far as I could see, from first to last they were solid masses of grass, as if the interior cavity or nest was to be excavated afterward, as doubtless it was. As they emerged from the pond they gradually assumed the shape of a miniature mountain, very bold and steep on the south side, and running down a long gentle grade to the surface of the water on the north.

One could see that the little architect hauled all his material up this easy slope, and thrust it out boldly around the other side. Every mouthful was distinctly defined. After they were two feet or more above the water, I expected each day to see that the finishing stroke had been given and the work brought to a close. But higher yet, said the builder. December drew near, the cold became threatening, and I was apprehensive that winter would suddenly shut down upon those unfinished nests. But the wise rats knew better than I did; they had received private advices from headquarters that I knew not of. Finally, about the 6th of December, the nests assumed completion; the northern incline was absorbed or carried up, and each structure became a strong massive cone, three or four feet high, the largest nest of the kind I had ever seen. Does it mean a severe winter? I inquired. An old farmer said it meant "high water," and he was right once, at least, for in a few days afterward we had the heaviest rainfall known in this section for half a century. The creeks rose to an almost unprecedented height. The sluggish pond became a seething, turbulent watercourse; gradually the angry element crept up the sides of these lake dwellings, till, when the rain ceased, about four o'clock they showed above the flood no larger than a man's hat. During the night the channel shifted till the main current swept over them, and next day not a vestige of the nests was to be seen; they had gone down-stream, as had many other dwellings of a less temporary character. The rats had built wisely, and would have been perfectly secure against any ordinary high water, but who can foresee a flood? The oldest traditions of their race did not run back to the time of such a visitation.

Nearly a week afterward another dwelling was begun, well away from the treacherous channel, but the architects did not work at it with much heart; the material was very scarce, the ice hindered, and before the basement-story was fairly finished, winter had the pond under his lock and key.

In other localities I noticed that where the nests were placed on the banks of streams, they were made secure against the floods by being built amid a small clump of bushes. When the fall of 1879 came, the muskrats were very tardy about beginning their house, laying the corner-stone—or the corner-sod-about December 1st, and continuing the work slowly and indifferently. On the 15th of the month the nest was not yet finished. This, I said, indicates a mild winter; and, sure enough, the season was one of the mildest known for many years. The rats had little use for their house.

Again, in the fall of 1880, while the weather-wise were wagging their heads, some forecasting a mild, some a severe winter, I watched with interest for a sign from my muskrats. About November 1st, a month earlier than the previous year, they began their nest, and worked at it with a will. They appeared to have just got tidings of what was coming. If I had taken the hint so palpably given, my celery would not have been frozen in the ground, and my apples caught in unprotected places. When the cold wave struck us, about November 20th, my four-legged "I-told-you-so's" had nearly completed their dwelling; it lacked only the ridge-board, so to speak; it needed a little "topping out," to give it a finished look. But this it never got. The winter had come to stay, and it waxed more and more severe, till the unprecedented cold of the last days of December must have astonished even the wise muskrats in their snug retreat. I approached their nest at this time, a white mound upon the white, deeply frozen surface of the pond, and wondered if there was any life in that apparent sepulcher. I thrust my walking-stick sharply into it, when there was a rustle and a splash into the water, as the occupant made his escape. What a damp basement that house has, I thought, and what a pity to rout out a peaceful neighbor out of his bed in this weather and into such a state of things as this! But water does not wet the muskrat; his fur is charmed, and not a drop penetrates it. Where the ground is favorable, the muskrats do not build these mound-like nests, but burrow into the bank a long distance, and establish their winter-quarters there.

Shall we not say, then, in view of the above facts, that this little creature is weather-wise? The hitting of the mark twice might be mere good luck; but three bull's-eyes in succession is not a mere coincidence; it is a proof of skill. The muskrat is not found in the Old World, which is a little singular, as other rats so abound there, and as those slow-going English streams especially, with their grassy banks, are so well suited to him. The water-rat of Europe is smaller, but of similar nature and habits. The muskrat does not hibernate like some rodents, but is pretty active all winter. In December I noticed in my walk where they had made excursions of a few yards to an orchard for frozen apples. One day, along a little stream, I saw a mink track amid those of the muskrat; following it up, I presently came to blood and other marks of strife upon the snow beside a stone wall. Looking in between the stones, I found the carcass of the luckless rat, with its head and neck eaten away. The mink had made a meal of him.

II. CHEATING THE SQUIRRELS

For the largest and finest chestnuts I had last fall I was indebted to the gray squirrels. Walking through the early October woods one day, I came upon a place where the ground was thickly strewn with very large unopened chestnut burs. On examination I found that every bur had been cut square off with about an inch of the stem adhering, and not one had been left on the tree. It was not accident, then, but design. Whose design? The squirrels'. The fruit was the finest I had ever seen in the woods, and some wise squirrel had marked it for his own. The burs were ripe, and had just begun to divide, not "threefold," but fourfold, "to show the fruit within." The squirrel that had taken all this pains had evidently reasoned with himself thus: "Now, these are extremely fine chestnuts, and I want them; if I wait till the burs open on the tree the crows and jays will be sure to carry off a great many of the nuts before they fall; then, after the wind has rattled out what remain, there are the mice, the chipmunks, the red squirrels, the raccoons, the grouse, to say nothing of the boys and the pigs, to come in for their share; so I will forestall events a little; I will cut off the burs when they have matured, and a few days of this dry October weather will cause everyone of them to open on the ground; I shall be on hand in the nick of time to gather up my nuts." The squirrel, of course, had to take the chances of a prowler like myself coming along, but he had fairly stolen a march on his neighbors. As I proceeded to collect and open the burs, I was half prepared to hear an audible protest from the trees about, for I constantly fancied myself watched by shy but jealous eyes. It is an interesting inquiry how the squirrel knew the burs would open if left to know, but thought the experiment worth trying.

The gray squirrel is peculiarly an American product, and might serve very well as a national emblem. The Old World can beat us on rats and mice, but we are far ahead on squirrels, having five or six species to Europe's one.

III. FOX AND HOUND

I stood on a high hill or ridge one autumn day and saw a hound run a fox through the fields far beneath me. What odors that fox must have shaken out of himself, I thought, to be traced thus easily, and how great their specific gravity not to have been blown away like smoke by the breeze! The fox ran a long distance down the hill, keeping within a few feet of a stone wall; then turned a right angle and led off for the mountain, across a plowed field and a succession of pasture lands. In about fifteen minutes the hound came in full blast with her nose in the air, and never once did she put it to the ground while in my sight. When she came to the stone wall she took the other side from that taken by the fox, and kept about the same distance from it, being thus separated several yards from his track, with the fence between her and it. At the point where the fox turned sharply to the left, the hound overshot a few yards, then wheeled, and feeling the air a moment with her nose, took up the scent again and was off on his trail as unerringly as fate. It seemed as if the fox must have sowed himself broadcast as he went along, and that his scent was so rank and heavy that it settled in the hollows and clung tenaciously to the bushes and crevices in the fence. I thought I ought to have caught a remnant of it as I passed that way some minutes later, but I did not. But I suppose it was not that the light-footed fox so impressed himself upon the ground he ran over, but that the sense of the hound was so keen. To her sensitive nose these tracks steamed like hot cakes, and they would not have cooled off so as to be undistinguishable for several hours. For the time being she had but one sense: her whole soul was concentrated in her nose.

It is amusing when the hunter starts out of a winter morning to see his hound probe the old tracks to determine how recent they are. He sinks his nose down deep in the snow so as to exclude the air from above, then draws a long full breath, giving sometimes an audible snort. If there remains the least effluvium of the fox the hound will detect it. If it be very slight it only sets his tail wagging; if it be strong it unloosens his tongue.

Such things remind one of the waste, the friction that is going on all about us, even when the wheels of life run the most smoothly. A fox cannot trip along the top of a stone wall so lightly but that he will leave enough of himself to betray his course to the hound for hours afterward. When the boys play "hare and hounds" the hare scatters bits of paper to give a clew to the pursuers, but he scatters himself much more freely if only our sight and scent were sharp enough to detect the fragments. Even the fish leave a trail in the water, and it is said the otter will pursue them by it. The birds make a track in the air, only their enemies hunt by sight rather than by scent. The fox baffles the hound most upon a hard crust of frozen snow; the scent will not hold to the smooth, bead-like granules.

Judged by the eye alone, the fox is the lightest and most buoyant creature that runs. His soft wrapping of fur conceals the muscular play and effort that is so obvious in the hound that pursues him, and he comes bounding along precisely as if blown by a gentle wind. His massive tail is carried as if it floated upon the air by its own lightness.

The hound is not remarkable for his fleetness, but how he will hang!—often running late into the night and sometimes till morning, from ridge to ridge, from peak to peak; now on the mountain, now crossing the valley, now playing about a large slope of uplying pasture fields. At times the fox has a pretty well-defined orbit, and the hunter knows where to intercept him. Again he leads off like a comet, quite beyond the system of hills and ridges upon which he was started, and his return is entirely a matter of conjecture; but if the day be not more than half spent, the chances are that the fox will be back before night, though the sportsman's patience seldom holds out that long.

The hound is a most interesting dog. How solemn and long-visaged he is—how peaceful and well-disposed! He is the Quaker among dogs. All the viciousness and currishness seem to have been weeded out of him; he seldom quarrels, or fights, or plays, like other dogs. Two strange hounds, meeting for the first time, behave as civilly toward each other as if two men. I know a hound that has an ancient, wrinkled, human, far-away look that reminds one of the bust of Homer among the Elgin marbles. He looks like the mountains toward which his heart yearns so much.

The hound is a great puzzle to the farm dog; the latter, attracted by his baying, comes barking and snarling up through the fields bent on picking a quarrel; he intercepts the hound, snubs and insults and annoys him in every way possible, but the hound heeds him not; if the dog attacks him he gets away as best he can, and goes on with the trail; the cur bristles and barks and struts about for a while, then goes back to the house, evidently thinking the hound a lunatic, which he is for the time being—a monomaniac, the slave and victim of one idea. I saw the master of a hound one day arrest him in full course to give one of the hunters time to get to a certain runaway; the dog cried and struggled to free himself and would listen neither to threats nor caresses. Knowing he must be hungry, I offered him my lunch, but he would not touch it. I put it in his mouth, but he threw it contemptuously from him. We coaxed and petted and reassured him, but he was under a spell; he was bereft of all thought or desire but the one passion to pursue that trail.

IV. THE WOODCHUCK

Writers upon rural England and her familiar natural history make no mention of the marmot or woodchuck. In Europe this animal seems to be confined to high mountainous districts, as on our Pacific slope, burrowing near the snow line. It is more social or gregarious than the American species, living in large families like our prairie-dog. In the Middle and Eastern States our woodchuck takes the place, in some respects, of the English rabbit, burrowing in every hillside and under every stone wall and jutting ledge and large bowlder, from whence it makes raids upon the grass and clover and sometimes upon the garden vegetables. It is quite solitary in its habits, seldom more than one inhabiting the same den, unless it be a mother and her young. It is not now so much a wood chuck as a field chuck. Occasionally, however, one seems to prefer the woods, and is not seduced by the sunny slopes and the succulent grass, but feeds, as did his fathers before him, upon roots and twigs, the bark of young trees, and upon various wood plants.

One summer day, as I was swimming across a broad, deep pool in the creek in a secluded place in the woods, I saw one of these sylvan chucks amid the rocks but a few feet from the edge of the water where I proposed to touch. He saw my approach, but doubtless took me for some water-fowl, or for some cousin of his of the muskrat tribe; for he went on with his feeding, and regarded me not till I paused within ten feet of him and lifted myself up. Then he did not know me; having, perhaps, never seen Adam in his simplicity, but he twisted his nose around to catch my scent; and the moment he had done so he sprang like a jumping-jack and rushed into his den with the utmost precipitation.

The woodchuck is the true serf among our animals; he belongs to the soil, and savors of it. He is of the earth, earthy. There is generally a decided odor about his dens and lurking-places, but it is not at all disagreeable in the clover-scented air, and his shrill whistle, as he takes to his hole or defies the farm dog from the interior of the stone wall, is a pleasant summer sound. In form and movement the woodchuck is not captivating. His body is heavy and flabby. Indeed, such a flaccid, fluid, pouchy carcass, I have never before seen. It has absolutely no muscular tension or rigidity, but is as baggy and shaky as a skin filled with water. Let the rifleman shoot one while it lies basking on a sidelong rock, and its body slumps off, and rolls and spills down the hill, as if it were a mass of bowels only. The legs of the woodchuck are short and stout, and made for digging rather than running. The latter operation he performs by short leaps, his belly scarcely clearing the ground. For a short distance he can make very good time, but he seldom trusts himself far from his hole, and when surprised in that predicament, makes little effort to escape, but, grating his teeth, looks the danger squarely in the face.

I knew a farmer in New York who had a very large bob-tailed churn-dog by the name of Cuff. The farmer kept a large dairy and made a great deal of butter, and it was the business of Cuff to spend nearly the half of each summer day treading the endless round of the churning-machine. During the remainder of the day he had plenty of time to sleep, and rest, and sit on his hips and survey the landscape. One day, sitting thus, he discovered a woodchuck about forty rods from the house, on a steep side-hill, feeding about near his hole, which was beneath a large rock. The old dog, forgetting his stiffness, and remembering the fun he had had with woodchucks in his earlier days, started off at his highest speed, vainly hoping to catch this one before he could get to his hole. But the woodchuck, seeing the dog come laboring up the hill, sprang to the mouth of his den, and, when his pursuer was only a few rods off, whistled tauntingly and went in. This occurred several times, the old dog marching up the hill, and then marching down again, having had his labor for his pains. I suspect that he revolved the subject in his mind while he revolved the great wheel of the churning-machine, and that some turn or other brought him a happy thought, for next time he showed himself a strategist. Instead of giving chase to the woodchuck when first discovered, he crouched down to the ground, and, resting his head on his paws, watched him. The woodchuck kept working away from the hole, lured by the tender clover, but, not unmindful of his safety, lifted himself up on his haunches every few moments and surveyed the approaches. Presently, after the woodchuck had let himself down from one of these attitudes of observation, and resumed his feeding, Cuff started swiftly but stealthily up the hill, precisely in the attitude of a cat when she is stalking a bird. When the woodchuck rose up again, Cuff was perfectly motionless and half hid by the grass. When he again resumed his clover, Cuff sped up the hill as before, this time crossing a fence, but in a low place, and so nimbly that he was not discovered. Again the wood chuck was on the outlook, again Cuff was motionless and hugging the ground. As the dog nears his victim he is partially hidden by a swell in the earth, but still the woodchuck from his outlook reports "all right," when Cuff, having not twice as far to run as the 'chuck, throws all stealthiness aside and rushes directly for the hole. At that moment the woodchuck discovers his danger, and, seeing that it is a race for life, leaps as I never saw marmot leap before. But he is two seconds too late, his retreat is cut off, and the powerful jaws of the old dog close upon him.

The next season Cuff tried the same tactics again with like success; but when the third woodchuck had taken up his abode at the fatal hole, the old churner's wits and strength had begun to fail him, and he was baffled in each attempt to capture the animal.

The woodchuck always burrows on a side-hill. This enables him to guard against being drowned out, by making the termination of the hole higher than the entrance. He digs in slantingly for about two or three feet, then makes a sharp upward turn and keeps nearly parallel with the surface of the ground for a distance of eight or ten feet farther, according to the grade. Here he makes his nest and passes the winter, holing up in October or November and coming out again in April. This is a long sleep, and is rendered possible only by the amount of fat with which the system has become stored during the summer. The fire of life still burns, but very faintly and slowly, as with the draughts all closed and the ashes heaped up. Respiration is continued, but at longer intervals, and all the vital processes are nearly at a standstill. Dig one out during hibernation (Audubon did so), and you find it a mere inanimate ball, that suffers itself to be moved and rolled about without showing signs of awakening. But bring it in by the fire, and it presently unrolls and opens its eyes, and crawls feebly about, and if left to itself will seek some dark hole or corner, roll itself up again, and resume its former condition.

The Heart of the Southern Catskills

On looking at the southern and more distant Catskills from the Hudson River on the east, or on looking at them from the west from some point of vantage in Delaware County, you see, amid the group of mountains, one that looks like the back and shoulders of a gigantic horse. The horse has got his head down grazing; the shoulders are high, and the descent from them down his neck very steep; if he were to lift up his head, one sees that it would be carried far above all other peaks, and that the noble beast might gaze straight to his peers in the Adirondacks or the White Mountains. But the lowered head never comes up; some spell or enchantment keeps it down there amid the mighty herd; and the high round shoulders and the smooth strong back of the steed are alone visible. The peak to which I refer is Slide Mountain, the highest of the Catskills by some two hundred feet, and probably the most inaccessible; certainly the hardest to get a view of, it is hedged about so completely by other peaks, — the greatest mountain of them all, and apparently the least willing to be seen; only at a distance of thirty or forty miles is it seen to stand up above all other peaks. It takes its name from a landslide which occurred many years ago down its steep northern side, or down the neck of the grazing steed. The mane of spruce and balsam fir was stripped away for many hundred feet, leaving a long gray streak visible from afar.

Slide Mountain is the centre and the chief of the southern Catskills. Streams flow from its base, and from the base of its subordinates, to all points of the compass,— the Rondout and the Neversink to the south; the Beaverkill to the west; the Esopus to the north; and several lesser streams to the east. With its summit as the centre, a radius of ten miles would include within the circle described but very little cultivated land; only a few poor, wild farms in some of the numerous valleys. The soil is poor, a mixture of gravel and clay, and is subject to slides. It lies in the valleys in ridges and small hillocks, as if dumped there from a huge cart. The tops of the southern Catskills are all capped with a kind of conglomerate, or "pudden stone,"— a rock of cemented quartz pebbles which underlies the coal measures. This rock disintegrates under the action of the elements, and the sand and gravel which result are carried into the valleys and make up the most of the soil. From the northern Catskills, so far as I know them, this rock has been swept clean. Low down in the valleys the old red sandstone crops out, and, as you go west into Delaware County, in many places it alone remains and makes up most of the soil, all the superincumbent rock having been carried away.

Slide Mountain had been a summons and a challenge to me for many years. I had fished every stream that it nourished, and had camped in the wilderness on all sides of it, and whenever I had caught a glimpse of its summit I had promised myself to set foot there before another season should pass. But the seasons came and went, and my feet got no nimbler, and Slide Mountain no lower, until finally, one July, seconded by an energetic friend, we thought to bring Slide to terms by approaching him through the mountains on the east. With a farmer's son for guide we struck in by way of Weaver Hollow, and, after a long and desperate climb, contented ourselves with the Wittenberg, instead of Slide. The view from the Wittenberg is in many respects more striking, as you are perched immediately above a broader and more distant sweep of country, and are only about two hundred feet lower. You are here on the eastern brink of the southern Catskills, and the earth falls away at your feet and curves down through an immense stretch of forest till it joins the plain of Shokan, and thence sweeps away to the Hudson and beyond. Slide is southwest of you, six or seven miles distant, but is visible only when you climb into a treetop. I climbed and saluted him, and promised to call next time.

We passed the night on the Wittenberg, sleeping on the moss, between two decayed logs, with balsam boughs thrust into the ground and meeting and forming a canopy over us. In coming off the mountain in the morning we ran upon a huge porcupine, and I learned for the first time that the tail of a porcupine goes with a spring like a trap. It seems to be a set-lock; and you no sooner touch with the weight of a hair one of the quills than the tail leaps up in a most surprising manner, and the laugh is not on your side. The beast cantered along the path in my front, and I threw myself upon him, shielded by my roll of blankets. He submitted quietly to the indignity, and lay very still under my blankets, with his broad tail pressed close to the ground. This I proceeded to investigate, but had not fairly made a beginning when it went off like a trap, and my hand and wrist were full of quills. This caused me to let up on the creature, when it lumbered away till it tumbled down a precipice. The quills were quickly removed from my hand, when we gave chase. When we came up to him, he had wedged himself in between the rocks so that he presented only a back bristling with quills, with the tail lying in ambush below. He had chosen his position well, and seemed to defy us. After amusing ourselves by repeatedly springing his tail and receiving the quills in a rotten stick, we made a slip-noose out of a spruce root, and, after much manoeuvring, got it over his head and led him forth. In what a peevish, injured tone the creature did complain of our unfair tactics! He protested and protested, and whimpered and scolded like some infirm old man tormented by boys. His game after we led him forth was to keep himself as much as possible in the shape of a ball, but with two sticks and the cord we finally threw him over on his back and exposed his quill-less and vulnerable under side, when he fairly surrendered and seemed to say, "Now you may do with me as you like." His great chisel-like teeth, which are quite as formidable as those of the woodchuck, he does not appear to use at all in his defense, but relies entirely upon his quills, and when those fail him, he is done for.

After amusing ourselves with him awhile longer, we released him and went on our way. The trail to which we had committed ourselves led us down into Woodland Valley, a retreat which so took my eye by its fine trout brook, its superb mountain scenery, and its sweet seclusion, that I marked it for my own, and promised myself a return to it at no distant day. This promise I kept, and pitched my tent there twice during that season. Both occasions were a sort of laying siege to Slide, but we only skirmished with him at a distance; the actual assault was not undertaken. But the following year, reinforced by two other brave climbers, we determined upon the assault, and upon making it from this the most difficult side. The regular way is by Big Ingin Valley, where the climb is comparatively easy, and where it is often made by women. But from Woodland Valley only men may essay the ascent. Larkins is the upper inhabitant, and from our camping-ground near his clearing we set out early one June morning.

One would think nothing could be easier to find than a big mountain, especially when one is encamped upon a stream which he knows springs out of its very loins. But for some reason or other we had got an idea that Slide Mountain was a very slippery customer and must be approached cautiously. We had tried from several points in the valley to get a view of it, but were not quite sure we had seen its very head. When on the Wittenberg, a neighboring peak, the year before, I had caught a brief glimpse of it only by climbing a dead tree and craning up for a moment from its topmost branch. It would seem as if the mountain had taken every precaution to shut itself off from a near view. It was a shy mountain, and we were about to stalk it through six or seven miles of primitive woods, and we seemed to have some unreasonable fear that it might elude us. We had been told of parties who had essayed the ascent from this side, and had returned baffled and bewildered. In a tangle of primitive woods, the very bigness of the mountain baffles one. It is all mountain; whichever way you turn—and one turns sometimes in such cases before he knows it—the foot finds a steep and rugged ascent.

The eye is of little service; one must be sure of his bearings and push boldly on and up. One is not unlike a flea upon a great shaggy beast, looking for the animal's head; or even like a much smaller and much less nimble creature,—he may waste his time and steps, and think he has reached the head when he is only upon the rump. Hence I questioned our host, who had several times made the ascent, closely. Larkins laid his old felt hat upon the table, and, placing one hand upon one side of it and the other upon the other, said: "There Slide lies, between the two forks of the stream, just as my hat lies between my two hands. David will go with you to the forks, and then you will push right on up." But Larkins was not right, though he had traversed all those mountains many times over. The peak we were about to set out for did not lie between the forks, but exactly at the head of one of them; the beginnings of the stream are in the very path of the slide, as we afterward found. We broke camp early in the morning, and with our blankets strapped to our backs and rations in our pockets for two days, set out along an ancient and in places an obliterated bark road that followed and crossed and recrossed the stream. The morning was bright and warm, but the wind was fitful and petulant, and I predicted rain. What a forest solitude our obstructed and dilapidated wood-road led us through! five miles of primitive woods before we came to the forks, three miles before we came to the "burnt shanty," a name merely,—no shanty there now for twenty-five years past. The ravages of the barkpeelers were still visible, now in a space thickly strewn with the soft and decayed trunks of hemlock-trees, and overgrown with wild cherry, then in huge mossy logs scattered through the beech and maple woods. Some of these logs were so soft and mossy that one could sit or recline upon them as upon a sofa.

But the prettiest thing was the stream soliloquizing in such musical tones there amid the moss-covered rocks and boulders. How clean it looked, what purity! Civilization corrupts the streams as it corrupts the Indian; only in such remote woods can you now see a brook in all its original freshness and beauty. Only the sea and the mountain forest brook are pure; all between is contaminated more or less by the work of man. An ideal trout brook was this, now hurrying, now loitering, now deepening around a great boulder, now gliding evenly over a pavement of green-gray stone and pebbles; no sediment or stain of any kind, but white and sparkling as snow-water, and nearly as cool. Indeed, the water of all this Catskill region is the best in the world. For the first few days, one feels as if he could almost live on the water alone; he cannot drink enough of it. In this particular it is indeed the good Bible land, "a land of brooks of water, of fountains and depths that spring out of valleys and hills."

Near the forks we caught, or thought we caught, through an opening, a glimpse of Slide. Was it Slide? was it the head, or the rump, or the shoulder of the shaggy monster we were in quest of? At the forks there was a bewildering maze of underbrush and great trees, and the way did not seem at all certain; nor was David, who was then at the end of his reckoning, able to reassure us. But in assaulting a mountain, as in assaulting a fort, boldness is the watchword. We pressed forward, following a line of blazed trees for nearly a mile, then, turning to the left, began the ascent of the mountain. It was steep, hard climbing. We saw numerous marks of both bears and deer; but no birds, save at long intervals the winter wren flitting here and there, and darting under logs and rubbish like a mouse. Occasionally its gushing, lyrical song would break the silence. After we had climbed an hour or two, the clouds began to gather, and presently the rain began to come down. This was discouraging; but we put our backs up against trees and rocks, and waited for the shower to pass.

"They were wet with the showers of the mountain, and embraced the rocks for want of shelter," as they did in Job's time. But the shower was light and brief, and we were soon under way again. Three hours from the forks brought us out on the broad level back of the mountain upon which Slide, considered as an isolated peak, is reared. After a time we entered a dense growth of spruce which covered a slight depression in the table of the mountain. The moss was deep, the ground spongy, the light dim, the air hushed. The transition from the open, leafy woods to this dim, silent, weird grove was very marked. It was like the passage from the street into the temple. Here we paused awhile and ate our lunch, and refreshed ourselves with water gathered from a little well sunk in the moss.

The quiet and repose of this spruce grove proved to be the calm that goes before the storm. As we passed out of it, we came plump upon the almost perpendicular battlements of Slide. The mountain rose like a huge, rock-bound fortress from this plain-like expanse. It was ledge upon ledge, precipice upon precipice, up which and over which we made our way slowly and with great labor, now pulling ourselves up by our hands, then cautiously finding niches for our feet and zigzagging right and left from shelf to shelf. This northern side of the mountain was thickly covered with moss and lichens, like the north side of a tree. This made it soft to the foot, and broke many a slip and fall. Everywhere a stunted growth of yellow birch, mountain-ash, and spruce and fir opposed our progress. The ascent at such an angle with a roll of blankets on your back is not unlike climbing a tree: every limb resists your progress and pushes you back; so that when we at last reached the summit, after twelve or fifteen hundred feet of this sort of work, the fight was about all out of the best of us. It was then nearly two o'clock, so that we had been about seven hours in coming seven miles.

Here on the top of the mountain we overtook spring, which had been gone from the valley nearly a month. Red clover was opening in the valley below, and wild strawberries just ripening; on the summit the yellow birch was just hanging out its catkins, and the claytonia, or spring-beauty, was in bloom. The leaf-buds of the trees were just bursting, making a faint mist of green, which, as the eye swept downward, gradually deepened until it became a dense, massive cloud in the valleys. At the foot of the mountain the clintonia, or northern green lily, and the low shadbush were showing their berries, but long before the top was reached they were found in bloom. I had never before stood amid blooming claytonia, a flower of April, and looked down upon a field that held ripening strawberries. Every thousand feet elevation seemed to make about ten days' difference in the vegetation, so that the season was a month or more later on the top of the mountain than at its base. A very pretty flower which we began to meet with well up on the mountain-side was the painted trillium, the petals white, veined with pink.

The low, stunted growth of spruce and fir which clothes the top of Slide has been cut away over a small space on the highest point, laying open the view on nearly all sides. Here we sat down and enjoyed our triumph. We saw the world as the hawk or the balloonist sees it when he is three thousand feet in the air. How soft and flowing all the outlines of the hills and mountains beneath us looked! The forests dropped down and undulated away over them, covering them like a carpet. To the east we looked over the near-by Wittenberg range to the Hudson and beyond; to the south, Peak-o'-Moose, with its sharp crest, and Table Mountain, with its long level top, were the two conspicuous objects; in the west, Mt. Graham and Double Top, about three thousand eight hundred feet each, arrested the eye; while in our front to the north we looked over the top of Panther Mountain to the multitudinous peaks of the northern Catskills. All was mountain and forest on every hand. Civilization seemed to have done little more than to have scratched this rough, shaggy surface of the earth here and there. In any such view, the wild, the aboriginal, the geographical greatly predominate. The works of man dwindle, and the original features of the huge globe come out. Every single object or point is dwarfed; the valley of the Hudson is only a wrinkle in the earth's surface. You discover with a feeling of surprise that the great thing is the earth itself, which stretches away on every hand so far beyond your ken.

The Arabs believe that the mountains steady the earth and hold it together; but they have only to get on the top of a high one to see how insignificant mountains are, and how adequate the earth looks to get along without them. To the imaginative Oriental people, mountains seemed to mean much more than they do to us. They were sacred; they were the abodes of their divinities. They offered their sacrifices upon them. In the Bible, mountains are used as a symbol of that which is great and holy. Jerusalem is spoken of as a holy mountain. The Syrians were beaten by the Children of Israel because, said they, "their gods are gods of the hills; therefore were they stronger than we." It was on Mount Horeb that God appeared to Moses in the burning bush, and on Sinai that He delivered to him the law. Josephus says that the Hebrew shepherds never pasture their flocks on Sinai, believing it to be the abode of Jehovah. The solitude of mountain-tops is peculiarly impressive, and it is certainly easier to believe the Deity appeared in a burning bush there than in the valley below. When the clouds of heaven, too, come down and envelop the top of the mountain,—how such a circumstance must have impressed the old God-fearing Hebrews! Moses knew well how to surround the law with the pomp and circumstance that would inspire the deepest awe and reverence.

But when the clouds came down and enveloped us on Slide Mountain, the grandeur, the solemnity, were gone in a twinkling; the portentous-looking clouds proved to be nothing but base fog that wet us and extinguished the world for us. How tame, and prosy, and humdrum the scene instantly became! But when the fog lifted, and we looked from under it as from under a just-raised lid, and the eye plunged again like an escaped bird into those vast gulfs of space that opened at our feet, the feeling of grandeur and solemnity quickly came back.

The first want we felt on the top of Slide, after we had got some rest, was a want of water. Several of us cast about, right and left, but no sign of water was found. But water must be had, so we all started off deliberately to hunt it up. We had not gone many hundred yards before we chanced upon an ice-cave beneath some rocks,—vast masses of ice, with crystal pools of water near. This was good luck, indeed, and put a new and a brighter face on the situation.

Slide Mountain enjoys a distinction which no other mountain in the State, so far as is known, does,—it has a thrush peculiar to itself. This thrush was discovered and described by Eugene P. Bicknell, of New York, in 1880, and has been named Bicknell's thrush. A better name would have been Slide Mountain thrush, as the bird so far has been found only on this mountain.[1] I did not see or hear it upon the Wittenberg, which is only a few miles distant, and only two hundred feet lower. In its appearance to the eye among the trees, one would not distinguish it from the gray-cheeked thrush of Baird, or the olive-backed thrush, but its song is totally different. The moment I heard it I said, "There is a new bird, a new thrush," for the quality of all thrush songs is the same. A moment more, and I knew it was Bicknell's thrush. The song is in a minor key, finer, more attenuated, and more under the breath than that of any other thrush. It seemed as if the bird was blowing in a delicate, slender, golden tube, so fine and yet so flute-like and resonant the song appeared. At times it was like a musical whisper of great sweetness and power. The birds were numerous about the summit, but we saw them nowhere else. No other thrush was seen, though a few times during our stay I caught a mere echo of the hermit's song far down the mountain-side. A bird I was not prepared to see or to hear was the black-poll warbler, a bird usually found much farther north, but here it was, amid the balsam firs, uttering its simple, lisping song.

The rocks on the tops of these mountains are quite sure to attract one's attention, even if he have no eye for such things. They are masses of light reddish conglomerate, composed of round wave-worn quartz pebbles. Every pebble has been shaped and polished upon some ancient seacoast, probably the Devonian. The rock disintegrates where it is most exposed to the weather, and forms a loose sandy and pebbly soil. These rocks form the floor of the coal formation, but in the Catskill region only the floor remains; the superstructure has never existed, or has been swept away; hence one would look for a coal mine here over his head in the air, rather than under his feet.

This rock did not have to climb up here as we did; the mountain stooped and took it upon its back in the bottom of the old seas, and then got lifted up again. This happened so long ago that the memory of the oldest inhabitants of these parts yields no clew to the time.

A pleasant task we had in reflooring and reroofing the log-hut with balsam boughs against the night. Plenty of small balsams grew all about, and we soon had a huge pile of their branches in the old hut. What a transformation, this fresh green carpet and our fragrant bed, like the deep-furred robe of some huge animal, wrought in that dingy interior! Two or three things disturbed our sleep. A cup of strong beef-tea taken for supper disturbed mine; then the porcupines kept up such a grunting and chattering near our heads, just on the other side of the log, that sleep was difficult. In my wakeful mood I was a good deal annoyed by a little rabbit that kept whipping in at our dilapidated door and nibbling at our bread and hardtack. He persisted even after the gray of the morning appeared. Then about four o'clock it began gently to rain. I think I heard the first drop that fell. My companions were all in sound sleep. The rain increased, and gradually the sleepers awoke. It was like the tread of an advancing enemy which every ear had been expecting. The roof over us was of the poorest, and we had no confidence in it. It was made of the thin bark of spruce and balsam, and was full of hollows and depressions. Presently these hollows got full of water, when there was a simultaneous downpour of bigger and lesser rills upon the sleepers beneath. Said sleepers, as one man, sprang up, each taking his blanket with him; but by the time some of the party had got themselves stowed away under the adjacent rock, the rain ceased. It was little more than the dissolving of the nightcap of fog which so often hangs about these heights. With the first appearance of the dawn I had heard the new thrush in the scattered trees near the hut,—a strain as fine as if blown upon a fairy flute, a suppressed musical whisper from out the tops of the dark spruces. Probably never did there go up from the top of a great mountain a smaller song to greet the day, albeit it was of the purest harmony. It seemed to have in a more marked degree the quality of interior reverberation than any other thrush song I had ever heard. Would the altitude or the situation account for its minor key? Loudness would avail little in such a place. Sounds are not far heard on a mountain-top; they are lost in the abyss of vacant air. But amid these low, dense, dark spruces, which make a sort of canopied privacy of every square rod of ground, what could be more in keeping than this delicate musical whisper? It was but the soft hum of the balsams, interpreted and embodied in a bird's voice.

It was the plan of two of our companions to go from Slide over into the head of the Rondout, and thence out to the railroad at the little village of Shokan, an unknown way to them, involving nearly an all-day pull the first day through a pathless wilderness. We ascended to the topmost floor of the tower, and from my knowledge of the topography of the country I pointed out to them their course, and where the valley of the Rondout must lie. The vast stretch of woods, when it came into view from under the foot of Slide, seemed from our point of view very uniform. It swept away to the southeast, rising gently toward the ridge that separates Lone Mountain from Peak-o'-Moose, and presented a comparatively easy problem. As a clew to the course, the line where the dark belt or saddle-cloth of spruce, which covered the top of the ridge they were to skirt, ended, and the deciduous woods began, a sharp, well-defined line was pointed out as the course to be followed. It led straight to the top of the broad level-backed ridge which connected two higher peaks, and immediately behind which lay the headwaters of the Rondout. Having studied the map thoroughly, and possessed themselves of the points, they rolled up their blankets about nine o'clock, and were off, my friend and I purposing to spend yet another day and night on Slide. As our friends plunged down into that fearful abyss, we shouted to them the old classic caution, "Be bold, be bold, -

be not too - bold." It required courage to make such a leap into the unknown, as I knew those young men were making, and it required prudence. A faint heart or a bewildered head, and serious consequences might have resulted. The theory of a thing is so much easier than the practice! The theory is in the air, the practice is in the woods; the eye, the thought, travel easily where the foot halts and stumbles. However, our friends made the theory and the fact coincide; they kept the dividing line between the spruce and the birches, and passed over the ridge into the valley safely; but they were torn and bruised and wet by the showers, and made the last few miles of their journey on will and pluck alone, their last pound of positive strength having been exhausted in making the descent through the chaos of rocks and logs into the head of the valley. In such emergencies one overdraws his account; he travels on the credit of the strength he expects to gain when he gets his dinner and some sleep. Unless one has made such a trip himself (and I have several times in my life), he can form but a faint idea what it is like, — what a trial it is to the body, and what a trial it is to the mind. You are fighting a battle with an enemy in ambush. How those miles and leagues which your feet must compass lie hidden there in that wilderness; how they seem to multiply themselves; how they are fortified with logs, and rocks, and fallen trees; how they take refuge in deep gullies, and skulk behind unexpected eminences! Your body not only feels the fatigue of the battle, your mind feels the strain of the undertaking; you may miss your mark; the mountains may outmanoeuvre you. All that day, whenever I looked upon that treacherous wilderness, I thought with misgivings of those two friends groping their way there, and would have given much to know how it fared with them. Their concern was probably less than my own, because they were more ignorant of what was before them. Then there was just a slight shadow of a fear in my mind that I might have been in error about some points of the geography I had pointed out to them. But all was well, and the victory was won according to the campaign which I had planned. When we saluted our friends upon their own doorstep a week afterward, the wounds were nearly healed and the rents all mended.

When one is on a mountain-top, he spends most of the time in looking at the show he has been at such pains to see. About every hour we would ascend the rude lookout to take a fresh observation. With a glass I could see my native hills forty miles away to the northwest. I was now upon the back of the horse, yea, upon the highest point of his shoulders, which had so many times attracted my attention as a boy. We could look along his balsam-covered back to his rump, from which the eye glanced away down into the forests of the Neversink, and on the other hand plump down into the gulf where his head was grazing or drinking. During the day there was a grand procession of thunderclouds filing along over the northern Catskills, and letting down veils of rain and enveloping them. From such an elevation one has the same view of the clouds that he does from the prairie or the ocean. They do not seem to rest across and to be upborne by the hills, but they emerge out of the dim west, thin and vague, and grow and stand up as they get nearer and roll by him, on a level but invisible highway, huge chariots of wind and storm.

In the afternoon a thick cloud threatened us, but it proved to be the condensation of vapor that announces a cold wave. There was soon a marked fall in the temperature, and as night drew near it became pretty certain that we were going to have a cold time of it. The wind rose, the vapor above us thickened and came nearer, until it began to drive across the summit in slender wraiths, which curled over the brink and shut out the view. We became very diligent in getting in our night wood, and in gathering more boughs to calk up the openings in the hut. The wood we scraped together was a sorry lot, roots and stumps and branches of decayed spruce, such as we could collect without an axe, and some rags and tags of birch bark. The fire was built in one corner of the shanty, the smoke finding easy egress through large openings on the east side and in the roof over it. We doubled up the bed, making it thicker and more nest-like, and as darkness set in, stowed ourselves into it beneath our blankets. The searching wind found out every crevice about our heads and shoulders, and it was icy cold. Yet we fell asleep, and had slept about an hour when my companion sprang up in an unwonted state of excitement for so placid a man. His excitement was occasioned by the sudden discovery that what appeared to be a bar of ice was fast taking the place of his backbone. His teeth chattered, and he was convulsed with ague. I advised him to replenish the fire, and to wrap himself in his blanket and cut the liveliest capers he was capable of in so circumscribed a place. This he promptly did, and the thought of his wild and desperate dance there in the dim light, his tall form, his blanket flapping, his teeth chattering, the porcupines outside marking time with their squeals and grunts, still provokes a smile, though it was a serious enough matter at the time. After a while, the warmth came back to him, but he dared not trust himself again to the boughs; he fought the cold all night as one might fight a besieging foe. By carefully husbanding the fuel, the beleaguering enemy was kept at bay till morning came; but when morning did come, even the huge root he had used as a chair was consumed. Rolled in my blanket beneath a foot or more of balsam boughs, I had got some fairly good sleep, and was most of the time oblivious of the melancholy vigil of my friend. As we had but a few morsels of food left, and had been on rather short rations the day before, hunger was added to his other discomforts. At that time a letter was on the way to him from his wife, which contained this prophetic sentence: "I hope thee is not suffering with cold and hunger on some lone mountain-top."

Mr. Bicknell's thrush struck up again at the first signs of dawn, notwithstanding the cold. I could hear his penetrating and melodious whisper as I lay buried beneath the boughs. Presently I arose and invited my friend to turn in for a brief nap, while I gathered some wood and set the coffee brewing. With a brisk, roaring fire on, I left for the spring to fetch some water, and to make my toilet. The leaves of the mountain goldenrod, which everywhere

covered the ground in the opening, were covered with frozen particles of vapor, and the scene, shut in by fog, was chill and dreary enough.

We were now not long in squaring an account with Slide, and making ready to leave. Round pellets of snow began to fall, and we came off the mountain on the 10th of June in a November storm and temperature. Our purpose was to return by the same valley we had come. A well-defined trail led off the summit to the north; to this we committed ourselves. In a few minutes we emerged at the head of the slide that had given the mountain its name. This was the path made by visitors to the scene; when it ended, the track of the avalanche began; no bigger than your hand, apparently, had it been at first, but it rapidly grew, until it became several rods in width. It dropped down from our feet straight as an arrow until it was lost in the fog, and looked perilously steep. The dark forms of the spruce were clinging to the edge of it, as if reaching out to their fellows to save them. We hesitated on the brink, but finally cautiously began the descent. The rock was quite naked and slippery, and only on the margin of the slide were there any boulders to stay the foot, or bushy growths to aid the hand. As we paused, after some minutes, to select our course, one of the finest surprises of the trip awaited us: the fog in our front was swiftly whirled up by the breeze, like the drop-curtain at the theatre, only much more rapidly, and in a twinkling the vast gulf opened before us. It was so sudden as to be almost bewildering. The world opened like a book, and there were the pictures; the spaces were without a film, the forests and mountains looked surprisingly near; in the heart of the northern Catskills a wild valley was seen flooded with sunlight. Then the curtain ran down again, and nothing was left but the gray strip of rock to which we clung, plunging down into the obscurity. Down and down we made our way. Then the fog lifted again. It was Jack and his beanstalk renewed; new wonders, new views, awaited us every few moments, till at last the whole valley below us stood in the clear sunshine. We passed down a precipice, and there was a rill of water, the beginning of the creek that wound through the valley below; farther on, in a deep depression, lay the remains of an old snow-bank; Winter had made his last stand here, and April flowers were springing up almost amid his very bones. We did not find a palace, and a hungry giant, and a princess, at the end of our beanstalk, but we found a humble roof and the hospitable heart of Mrs. Larkins, which answered our purpose better. And we were in the mood, too, to have undertaken an eating-bout with any giant Jack ever discovered.

Of all the retreats I have found amid the Catskills, there is no other that possesses quite so many charms for me as this valley, wherein stands Larkins's humble dwelling; it is so wild, so quiet, and has such superb mountain views. In coming up the valley, you have apparently reached the head of civilization a mile or more lower down; here the rude little houses end, and you turn to the left into the woods. Presently you emerge into a clearing again, and before you rises the rugged and indented crest of Panther Mountain, and near at hand, on a low plateau, rises the humble roof of Larkins,—you get a picture of the Panther and of the homestead at one glance. Above the house hangs a high, bold cliff covered with forest, with a broad fringe of blackened and blasted tree-trunks, where the cackling of the great pileated woodpecker may be heard; on the left a dense forest sweeps up to the sharp spruce-covered cone of the Wittenberg, nearly four thousand feet high, while at the head of the valley rises Slide over all. From a meadow just back of Larkins's barn, a view may be had of all these mountains, while the terraced side of Cross Mountain bounds the view immediately to the east. Running from the top of Panther toward Slide one sees a gigantic wall of rock, crowned with a dark line of fir. The forest abruptly ends, and in its stead rises the face of this colossal rocky escarpment, like some barrier built by the mountain gods. Eagles might nest here. It breaks the monotony of the world of woods very impressively.

I delight in sitting on a rock in one of these upper fields, and seeing the sun go down behind Panther. The rapid-flowing brook below me fills all the valley with a soft murmur. There is no breeze, but the great atmospheric tide flows slowly in toward the cooling forest; one can see it by the motes in the air illuminated by the setting sun: presently, as the air cools a little, the tide turns and flows slowly out. The long, winding valley up to the foot of Slide, five miles of primitive woods, how wild and cool it looks, its one voice the murmur of the creek! On the Wittenberg the sunshine lingers long; now it stands up like an island in a sea of shadows, then slowly sinks beneath the wave. The evening call of a robin or a veery at his vespers makes a marked impression on the silence and the solitude.

The following day my friend and I pitched our tent in the woods beside the stream where I had pitched it twice before, and passed several delightful days, with trout in abundance and wild strawberries at intervals. Mrs. Larkins's cream-pot, butter-jar, and bread-box were within easy reach. Near the camp was an unusually large spring, of icy coldness, which served as our refrigerator. Trout or milk immersed in this spring in a tin pail would keep sweet four or five days. One night some creature, probably a lynx or a raccoon, came and lifted the stone from the pail that held the trout and took out a fine string of them, and ate them up on the spot, leaving only the string and one head. In August bears come down to an ancient and now brushy bark-peeling near by for blackberries. But the creature that most infests these backwoods is the porcupine. He is as stupid and indifferent as the skunk; his broad, blunt nose points a witless head. They are great gnawers, and will gnaw your house down if you do not look out. Of a summer evening they will walk coolly into your open door if not prevented. The most annoying animal to the camper-out in this region, and the one he needs to be most on the lookout for, is the cow. Backwoods cows and young cattle seem always to be famished for salt, and they will fairly lick the fisherman's clothes off his back, and his tent and equipage out of existence, if you give them a chance. On one occasion some wood-ranging heifers and steers that had been hovering around our camp for some days made a raid upon it when we were absent.

The tent was shut and everything snugged up, but they ran their long tongues under the tent, and, tasting something savory, hooked out John Stuart Mill's "Essays on Religion," which one of us had brought along, thinking to read in the woods. They mouthed the volume around a good deal, but its logic was too tough for them, and they contented themselves with devouring the paper in which it was wrapped. If the cattle had not been surprised at just that point, it is probable the tent would have gone down before their eager curiosity and thirst for salt.

The raid which Larkins's dog made upon our camp was amusing rather than annoying. He was a very friendly and intelligent shepherd dog, probably a collie. Hardly had we sat down to our first lunch in camp before he called on us. But as he was disposed to be too friendly, and to claim too large a share of the lunch, we rather gave him the cold shoulder. He did not come again; but a few evenings afterward, as we sauntered over to the house on some trifling errand, the dog suddenly conceived a bright little project. He seemed to say to himself, on seeing us, "There come both of them now, just as I have been hoping they would; now, while they are away, I will run quickly over and know what they have got that a dog can eat." My companion saw the dog get up on our arrival, and go quickly in the direction of our camp, and he said something in the cur's manner suggested to him the object of his hurried departure. He called my attention to the fact, and we hastened back. On cautiously nearing camp, the dog was seen amid the pails in the shallow water of the creek investigating them. He had uncovered the butter, and was about to taste it, when we shouted, and he made quick steps for home, with a very "kill-sheep" look. When we again met him at the house next day, he could not look us in the face, but sneaked off, utterly crest-fallen. This was a clear case of reasoning on the part of the dog, and afterward a clear case of a sense of guilt from wrong-doing. The dog will probably be a man before any other animal.

1907 portrait by Orlando Rouland.

About the Editor

Edward Renehan is the author more than 20 books, the first of these being *John Burroughs: An American Naturalist* (1992), a work which remains the standard biography of the writer/naturalist. In addition to being an author, Renehan has pursued a long career as a publishing executive, including stints at John Wiley & Sons, St. Martin's Press, and Macmillan/MBCI where he served seven years as Director of Computer Publishing Programs. Renehan is currently managing director at New Street Communications, a firm he founded in 2010. He and his wife live in Wickford, Rhode Island, not far from Newport.

newstreetcommunications.com

www.ingramcontent.com/pod-product-compliance
Lightning Source LLC
LaVergne TN
LVHW051256080426
835509LV00020B/3005